Organizational Co-Dependence

Organizational
Co-Dependence

CAUSES AND CURES

J. Larry Goff and Patricia J. Goff

University Press of Colorado

Copyright © 1991 by the University Press of Colorado
P.O. Box 849
Niwot, Colorado 80544

The University Press of Colorado is a cooperative publishing enterprise supported, in part, by Adams State College, Colorado State University, Fort Lewis College, Mesa State College, Metropolitan State College of Denver, University of Colorado, University of Northern Colorado, University of Southern Colorado, and Western State College.

The paper used in this publication meets the minimum requirements of the American National Standard for Information Sciences—Permanence of Paper for Printed Library Materials. ANSI Z39.48–1984

Library of Congress Cataloging-in-Publication Data
Goff, J. Larry, 1937–
    Organizational co-dependence : causes and cures / J. Larry Goff
and Patricia J. Goff
        p. cm.
    Includes bibliographical references and index.
    ISBN 0-87081-224-6 (cloth). — ISBN 0-87081-244-0 (pbk.)
    1. Organizational behavior. I. Goff, Patricia J., 1942–   .
II. Title.
HD58.7.G46 1991
362.29'23 — dc20   91-26560
                                                        CIP

10 9 8 7 6 5 4 3 2 1

Design by Kristin Geishecker

For our two sons, Brad and Randy

Contents

PREFACE

We have wanted to write this book for some time, as the problem of organizational co-dependence has received only scant attention. Yet every time we went back to rewrite and make changes, we fond we had learned so much more that was important to include about this subject. Some writers have looked at alcoholism and other chemical addictions in the workplace. Others have explored the addictive process in organizations and in society at large. We have chosen to limit our discussion to co-dependency because it encompasses more people than do other addictions in that each addicted person has the potential to create several co-dependents.

We have seen a lot of pain and confusion in the workplace caused by co-dependency. Many people have no idea *why* they are unhappy, just that they *are* unhappy. Likewise, businesses have some notion that employees are having problems but have not been able to identify and deal with them. We believe that there are steps that can be taken to help both the employee and the organization escape some of the unfortunate effects that can happen to each of them. These begin with an understanding of the problem and then taking measures to correct it.

We have placed most of the focus on Chapter 3, which deals with what we have termed "Organizational Co-Dependency," and on Chapter 10, which discusses "Recovery." Some material about personal recovery used in Chapter 10 we wrote originally for the *Personnel Journal* and is reprinted here by permission and through an agreement between the authors and that publication.

We hope this book will help some of you either as managers or employees as well as others interested in addictive behavior.

CHAPTER 1

INTRODUCTION

Co-dependency is everywhere today. So it should not come as a surprise when we can find it in modern business organizations. The only really puzzling thing is that it has taken so long to put a label on it, and even more curious is that to a large extent we still do not know what to do about it.

Example. Susan worked part time in a retail store. She had been at this job for about six months when she began having some real depression on workdays. She would wake up with an anxious feeling, not sure if she even wanted to go to work. She was confused about why she felt this way. She did not feel like this on her days off. Things were never consistent at work. One day her boss would be great and would buy everyone lunch; the next day she wondered why everyone was so lazy. Susan was probably being exposed to a large dose of co-dependent behavior from her boss and was reacting to the up and down moods. Her mood was up when her boss felt good, and down when her boss had a bad day. She never knew when she went to work in the morning what the day was going to be like.

Example. Sam had only had one job. He got out of high school and went to work for a company and stayed there for the next fifteen years. During that time the company was sold to a large conglomerate. Over the first few months under new management, most of the old employees were fired. They were let go for a variety of reasons. Nobody could understand exactly what was happening. But Sam lived in almost constant fear that any day might be his last on the job. He had a lot of doubts about whether he could make it with another organization; after all, he had never worked anyplace else.

He thought about quitting, but that seemed disloyal. He tried to talk to his boss but got no real answers. The disruptive activity continued. Sam tried working harder. He only got paid for forty hours a week, but he was putting in eighty hours some weeks. He would show the new leadership he was worthy of keeping his job. Finally, it got to be too much, and Sam had to quit. The pressures on the job were disrupting his life at home.

Susan's and Sam's cases are not especially dramatic. They have some of the characteristics of co-dependents. What is happening to them, what they are experiencing and feeling, is fairly representative of what happens in the lives of many people at work every day. Yet we have had a hard time isolating the problem and defining it in such a way that it becomes treatable. Co-dependency as a separate and definable issue arrived on the psychological landscape fairly recently, more or less within the past ten years. Before that time, researchers and writers had described certain behavioral characteristics, traits, and personality patterns that caused people problems but had not yet categorized them under the heading of co-dependency.

For many years, treatment of chemically dependent persons concentrated solely upon the identified patient, i.e., the primary problem. Most of the time no attention was given to the family. During the 1950s and 1960s practitioners started to look at families as a system and began family therapy. As time went on, studies of addictions, which more or less paralleled the development of family therapy, provided a window through which the consistently unhealthy behaviors associated with families of chemically dependent persons were seen. Finally, researchers, writers, and counselors began to look at chemical dependency in the setting of family dynamics so that they were able to treat it as a family illness. At that point they were able to see what is now called co-dependency as a separate and describable issue. From this, alcohol and drug counselors started treating families at the same time they treated the addict.

They learned that many of the dynamics of co-dependency were the same as those of chemical dependency; the major difference was that in the chemically dependent person the addiction was to a substance, while in co-dependency it was generally to another person, attempting to control that person's behavior and accepting responsibility for consequences of such behavior.

As studies in this area continued, it was discovered that co-dependency was not limited only to those close to alcoholics and drug addicts. Instead, people who had other types of dysfunctional backgrounds, some free of substance abuse, were found to have similar problems and to exhibit the same types of characteristic behaviors. Today we know that co-dependency can develop from a variety of conditions. While it is commonly associated with addictions of some sort, such as substance addiction, workaholism, sexual addiction, compulsive gambling, and overeating, it can arise out of other types of emotionally repressive relationships. Some examples of these relationships come from families that are too strict, overly religious, that communicate poorly, or where there has been abuse of some sort.

Dr. Timmen Cermak is a San Francisco psychiatrist who has been a researcher and practitioner for some time in the area of co-dependency, as well as a founding board member, president, and chair of the National Association for Children of Alcoholics. He has proposed a model for inclusion in the American Psychiatric Association's *Diagnostic and Statistical Manual of Mental Disorders* (see Appendix A). We agree with Dr. Cermak that co-dependency is a serious enough problem to deserve classification as a primary mental disorder (1986). He has also stated it should be described as a disease entity (1986, p. 3). If co-dependency remains untreated, it causes maladaptive behaviors and coping problems in the day-to-day lives of its victims. (Cermak also points out that the behavior itself is not new and suggests the myth of Narcissus and Echo as a prototype for co-dependency.)

Co-dependency is another variation of addictive behavior (Nakken 1988). We define *co-dependency* as the condition wherein one person tries to control another (or him or herself) and to be responsible for the consequences of the behavior of that other person. This description may seem short and not as all-inclusive as some other definitions since it does not address all of the manifestations of co-dependent behavior; it does, however, seem to capture the heart of the problem. This condition is distinguishable from that of the dependent person, although it is possible for one person to have both problems simultaneously. The dependent person is unable to make decisions and allows another person to take over this function. In the co-dependent, the opposite is true: the co-dependent wants to control someone else's life. However, both of these behaviors result in problems, some of which may occasionally intersect one another.

3

When we study and treat co-dependency, we use both the Chemical Dependency Model and the Psychotherapeutic Model. In the former case we are more concerned with *what* the person has to do each day in order to function. It is more health oriented and focuses on the here and now. In the latter model, therapists are looking at the *etiology*, the source of the problem, with a view toward correcting the underlying inconsistencies in the client's life that have caused the problem. This is more focused on pathology, i.e., the study of diseases, and looks more into the past of the individual.

Quite recently some writers, such as John Bradshaw, have begun to explore the issue of shame and how it affects those caught up in the web of addictive behavior. We believe that shame plays such an integral role in co-dependency that it is not possible now to discuss the origins of the problem without exploring the issue of shame-bound behavior. For our purposes here we will define shame as a constant, overwhelming feeling of inadequacy as a person.

After years of exploring the human psyche, psychology is just now beginning to address the concept of shame. It seems almost improbable that the whole area of human relations has largely ignored this obviously important and dynamic personality quality. Perhaps this has been due in part to the tendency to place shame and guilt under a common heading and to assume the two were more or less the same. Counselors have recently started to differentiate between these two similar, yet very different, parts of the human condition.

We believe that shame is important when we look at co-dependency and think co-dependency is relevant to business today. If this is true, then how do we fit shame into a discussion of co-dependency in a business setting? In many ways, we believe that the modern business organization is quite literally a factory for shame and the resulting co-dependency flowing from it. Much of what goes on inside a business tends to create, perpetuate, and exacerbate shame in its employees, as well as within its own corporate being. Was it intentionally designed that way? Probably not. There is no evidence that would lead to this conclusion. Yet, if a person were to set out this day deliberately to design an institution to breed and nurture feelings of shame, he could scarcely have succeeded better than with what presently exists. And with shame comes resulting co-dependency.

Anne Wilson Schaef in *When Society Becomes an Addict* (1987) and in her more recent *The Addictive Organization* (1988), with Diane Fassel, has suggested that society as a whole has become addicted and displays addictive qualities in very real and systematic fashions. As we shall see, this addictive process is deeply rooted in shame-bound feelings and behavior. Perhaps what has happened is that we have moved from the world of the individual to, as Schaef suggests, a societal condition. In turn, this may be accurately reflected in the modern business organization, which itself may be a model — a paradigm — of society as a whole.

While there is no question that a lot of people are affected by co-dependency, we think it is important to state our concern that many problems are presently getting indiscriminately lumped under this heading. With so many articles written in magazines and the popularity of this new term, it has become a convenient way to describe a variety of behaviors for which we cannot find other answers. Labeling a person or problem as co-dependent is not a panacea. We need to be very careful how it is used. We are trying to describe a disorder we believe has pathological implications and which has the capacity to do enormous damage to its victims, as well as the others who surround them, if it remains untreated.

Cermak suggests two types of co-dependency: primary and secondary (1990). In primary co-dependency, onset happens during the person's youth. Most of the issues this person will have to deal with relate to his own childhood. He really has no baseline, no sense of normalcy from his formative years, to which to return. This must be constructed for him in therapy. Secondary co-dependency occurs when onset happens during the adult years. This person may have had a very "normal" existence up to some point in his adult life. The primary objective with this person is to get him to detach from the person or object to which he is co-dependent. (*Detach* means the ability to put enough emotional distance between himself and the object of his co-dependency that he is no longer trying to control or be responsible for it.) This allows him to return to his baseline of normalcy and function reasonably well. Childhood discoveries are generally not indicated in his case.

This distinction is very significant in studying an organization as well. Some people bring their co-dependency with them into the organization (which we will call *personal* co-dependency), while others develop co-dependency from contact with the organization itself (which will be referred to as *organizational* co-dependency). With individuals, Cermak sees the two as distinguishable in point of time for onset. We believe a similar distinction can be made between the two types based upon the events causing the problem.

Personal and organizational co-dependency are very different issues. The factors causing each of them are different: causation for personal co-dependency follows a fairly orthodox pattern that has been explored by several writers; behaviors causing organizational co-dependency have not been fully explored, and we will look at some of the more important ones in Chapter 3. The way in which an individual handles co-dependency depends in large measure on which type of co-dependency it is. Likewise, businesses will take different approaches to help the affected individuals, depending on precipitating causes. Businesses can also see the role they play in the problem of organizational co-dependency and attempt to correct it.

In order to set the structure for the balance of the book, we want to outline the major points that will be addressed. We believe, as Bradshaw has suggested, that *personal* co-dependency commonly has its origins in childhood with issues of (1) abuse, (2) abandonment, (3) neglect, and (4) enmeshment (1988). From a business standpoint, *organizational* co-dependency, the type that results from contact with the organization, may be caused by: (1) depersonalization, (2) hierarchy, (3) comparisons and competition, (4) poor communication patterns, and (5) lack of appreciation for one's spiritual nature.

Both personal and organizational co-dependency cause shame. Shame, in turn, is the wheel we believe drives co-dependency. (For a detailed discussion, see John Bradshaw, *Bradshaw On: Healing the Shame That Binds You*, 1988.) Co-dependents, often victims of abusive behavior, have certain fairly common behavioral characteristics resulting from this shame: (1) placing others before self, (2) loss of identity, (3) unstable emotions, (4) compulsive behavior, (5) hypervigilance, (6) exaggerated mood swings, (7) anxiety, and (8) depression (Cermak 1986).

These behaviors are maintained by: (1) reinforcement, (2) repression, (3) association, and (4) distraction. Co-dependents attempt to cope with these behaviors through: (1) denial, (2) perfectionism, (3) blaming, and

(4) control. When all of these coping measures fail, the co-dependent feels more shame. Thus the problem has a cyclical nature and might appear as follows:

THE CYCLE OF CO-DEPENDENCY

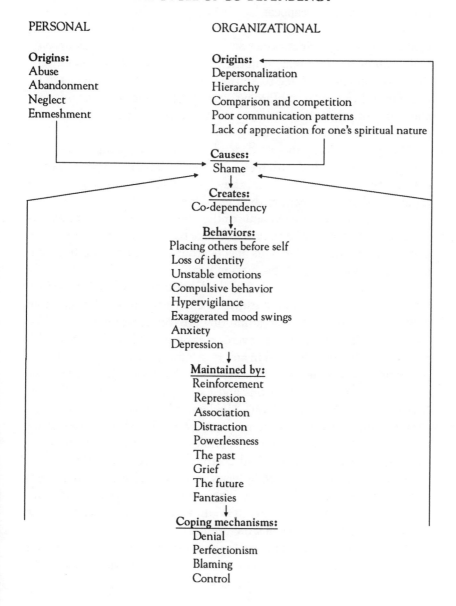

PERSONAL

ORGANIZATIONAL

Origins:
Abuse
Abandonment
Neglect
Enmeshment

Origins:
Depersonalization
Hierarchy
Comparison and competition
Poor communication patterns
Lack of appreciation for one's spiritual nature

Causes:
Shame

Creates:
Co-dependency

Behaviors:
Placing others before self
Loss of identity
Unstable emotions
Compulsive behavior
Hypervigilance
Exaggerated mood swings
Anxiety
Depression

Maintained by:
Reinforcement
Repression
Association
Distraction
Powerlessness
The past
Grief
The future
Fantasies

Coping mechanisms:
Denial
Perfectionism
Blaming
Control

Looking at this diagram, one can see that with the progress of co-dependency on a *personal* basis, certain conditions cause shame, which in turn creates co-dependency. As the circle closes and the cycle begins, the original causes (abuse, abandonment, neglect, and enmeshment) do not play a major or continuing role, although it is always possible for them to reappear later. On the other hand, with *organizational* co-dependency, the original causes (depersonalization, hierarchy, comparisons and competition, poor communication, and lack of spiritual awareness) often remain in the loop as the whole problem intensifies. In both cases we see there is a course of action that tends to be circular and mutually reinforcing, self-perpetuating in nature. It will continue until there is some intervention that specifically addresses the problem.

People caught up in a co-dependent existence spend a great deal of energy trying to deal with feelings resulting from it. To precisely the extent they are so preoccupied, they lose energy and thus productive capability that could benefit their employer.

Co-dependency as a dynamic of the human personality not only is a destroyer of people and their happiness, but also robs business of the best a person has to offer. This affects product quality and productive quantity. In short, it costs business money.

The purpose of this book is to look at some of what is presently happening in business and to study some of the patterns of destructive behavior that the modern organization both tolerates and nurtures. We will also explore some ways to overcome these problems both from the perspective of the individual in an organizational setting and from the point of view of the organization itself. Our theoretical framework comes from our interpretations and extrapolations of Anne Wilson Schaef, John Bradshaw, Craig Nakken, Merle Fossum Marilyn J. Mason, Tim Cermak, and the many other writers who have explored family systems, groups, addictions, and co-dependency, as well as our own experiences and those of others that have been shared with us.

Organizations have specific ways in which they create and deal with the issue of co-dependency. They develop some of these characteristics in much the same way as do individuals, while others appear unique to the organizational structure itself.

Our laboratory is the modern business organization as seen through our eyes and those of others. This is not meant to be an authoritative exploration or a controlled study of the phenomena we are attempting to describe, but rather a jumping-off place for more study and investigation. Likewise, this book is not written to communicate exclusively with academia; hopefully it is designed to be a practitioner's guide, user-friendly, something that can be read and understood by most people.

We believe a look at co-dependency in the business setting is important and necessary and has not really yet been done. As we talk to people, counsel with them, and do consulting, we find many people who will come forward and say something like, "You know, that is absolutely right. Let me tell you what happened to me. You can use my experience the next time you write something because it is real."

And so we now are going to share some of that with you.

CHAPTER 2

ORIGINS OF PERSONAL SHAME

Where does shame originate? We believe that it is impossible for shame to begin in a vacuum; it finds its genesis in some type of relationship. Such a relationship may be with another person, an object, an organization, or an event. It is the result of transactions taking place.

Shame may arise from one significant event, but most often develops insidiously through a series of transactions over a period of time. The denial invariably surrounding this masks the associated uncomfortable feelings and keeps shame and its resulting negative feelings, thoughts, and behaviors out of the consciousness of the affected person. Thus, as the shame deepens, the victim is largely unaware of what is happening.

Shame also can be the result of an inappropriate involvement of a person, event, organization, or object. Again these may be isolated or may be spread over a number of different events and circumstances in a person's life.

Whatever the causes, they must be something that represents value to the affected person. Transactions outside his scope of significance may become an inconvenience or perhaps an embarrassment, but they do not touch him in such a way as to create a deep psychological scar. Most shame-producing events happen within relationships with people closest to the victim.

In interpersonal relationships, Bradshaw has suggested the primary offenders are: (1) abuse, (2) abandonment, (3) neglect, and (4) enmeshment (1988).

ABUSE

Abuse is any attack on the personal identity of another person. This is a very broad definition but one which accurately describes abuse from an effect standpoint. That is, we are not so concerned with what causes the abuse as how it affects the victim. It may come in many forms: verbal, psychological, emotional, physical, or sexual. It is some act by the abuser that creates immediate shame in the victim. The statement being made by the abuser is that the victim does not count as a person. He or she is not entitled to even a small amount of dignity.

> **Example.** Physical and sexual abuse are reasonably easy to identify and describe. The more difficult type is emotional or psychological abuse. Perhaps the place we see it most commonly is in couples. We saw a situation recently where a husband and wife had some difficulties about whether she was going to work.
>
> Brad and Gwen had been married for three years when their problems first began. Gwen told Brad one evening that she wanted to go to work. Brad scoffed at the idea, telling her that she was not really qualified to do anything. From that point on he continued to ridicule her about her "silly ideas" of going to work and told her she was better suited to stay at home and try to keep the house decent for him. Gwen began to believe all of this, that she was in fact not really competent. This eventually translated into feelings of inadequacy.

This is abusive behavior. In analyzing it, one sees that Gwen is being shamed for even considering the idea she may be competent to work. This sort of situation is more common in marriages than people imagine. It seems to be some type of throwback to an earlier time when men felt they must be the breadwinner; if their wives worked, it was a personal reflection on their inadequacies to provide for the family. This is also interesting because it creates a double bind for the couple: if she works, he feels shamed; if she does not work, she feels shamed. We also see the same sort of dynamic in a business setting when one person begins to ridicule the work of another.

ABANDONMENT

Abandonment occurs when one person who has a responsibility to another moves away from and leaves the other. This may happen in a number of ways ranging from physical absence to emotional unavailability. The message being given is that you do not count in my world. In my world other things are more important to me. I do not care about you anymore.

> **Example.** This is where someone important moves off. It most commonly happens when one partner in a relationship deserts another. We see this in a business setting when one co-worker leaves another.
>
> Suzanne and Beverly had been co-workers for about two years. They had spent a lot of time with each other, eating lunch, taking short shopping trips during the lunch hour, meeting after work, etc. One day Beverly was no longer there for Suzanne. Beverly had found some new friends and did not want to include Suzanne in her new circle. Suzanne could not figure out what had happened. She felt totally rejected, cut off for no reason. She kept wondering what she had done wrong and what she could do to change so that Beverly would spend time with her again.

This type of situation is very frightening to the person who has been left behind. We also see this in other interpersonal relationships, especially romantic ones. When a person's partner or friend leaves for no reason, there is almost a knee-jerk reaction that "I have done something wrong." The problem becomes even more confusing and acute when the rejected person cannot figure out what has happened. The confusion builds on itself, and the result is that the person feels he just simply does not measure up as a human being. This is fertile ground for the seeds of shame-bound feelings and is a place where they often take root.

While this can happen at any age, the pattern for this type of distorted thinking often begins during adolescence, a time when young people are particularly sensitive to the attention of others. It is very frightening when a teenager does not feel accepted. Feelings bred at this time carry over to adult life and become the source of more shameful episodes.

NEGLECT

Neglect is seen when the actor and victim are still together, but the former does not fulfill his obligations or responsibilities to the latter.

This may range from simply neglecting food, care, etc., to becoming emotionally unavailable to someone who relies upon another. The message is that I do not want to be bothered with you. I am here, but you cannot have any access to me. This often happens without either player knowing it is going on. In looking at the treatment of families by the chemically dependent, one often sees an "I love you, go away" attitude. This double message is confusing to the recipient. Though one thing is heard, actions say something else.

> **Example.** In looking at one company, we saw the following situation. When Tom first came to work, he received a lot of attention from Alex, his boss. Alex called him for coffee, lunch, and occasionally for a drink after work. As time wore on, Alex became less attentive to Tom. Even when Tom would actively seek Alex out, he did not seem to be available. Tom became very concerned that he had done something wrong, something that had offended Alex. He was afraid to ask because it might confirm his fears. He began to see this in terms of failing in his job. After all, Alex was an important player in his business career. Actually, Alex had a pattern of this type of action. When a new person came to work, he went out of his way to make that person comfortable. He would give a lot of attention to the newcomer until he or she had gotten settled in. Then he would gradually move away and focus on other new people or other work. Alex saw himself as very caring and helpful. Tom did not know what to think. He was confused and afraid. His fear slowly converted into feelings that something was wrong with him.

In this particular situation, both players were acting in good faith. Alex simply did not understand some of the negative consequences of his own behavior. On the contrary, he thought he was being helpful. This happens a lot. There may be times when one person deliberately ignores another. We see this more in terms of abandonment than neglect, although it may occur in either case if the circumstances are right.

ENMESHMENT

Enmeshment is defined as the overinvolvement of one person in the life of another, or some event or object, where the former loses his own personality in the latter in an unhealthy manner. Enmeshment is, at best, very unhealthy; at worst it can become a pathological condition that is highly destructive.

Where one person tries to live through the life of another, both lose. The controller will experience frustration with his inability to control the other. This, in turn, translates into feelings of inadequacy and shame. The controlled person simply loses part of her identity. Since this is the very essence of shame, she cannot escape the net. It is a lose-lose situation.

This is probably the most elusive of all the types we discuss. It often looks like true concern and caring for another. Really it can be something very different. Sometimes it is hard to distinguish between what is true caring and what is in fact enmeshment. Perhaps the easiest way to do this is to look at motives: if the person is doing something that helps the other to live and grow as a full human being, it is probably altruistic; if he is doing it to benefit himself or control the other person, it may qualify as enmeshment. We see partners and parents often caught in this trap. It is a natural place for them to be since they have both a personal and socially imposed need to care for those close to them.

> **Example.** There is another business situation we see as almost classic enmeshment.
>
> Chris was a very successful businessman. He had built up his own business and then began to expand into other areas. As he did this, he found he was unable to run all of his enterprises. So he hired Chuck to be his good right hand, to take over the operation of two of these businesses. Chuck was very competent. He worked hard, but as time went by he became very frustrated because Chris just would not keep his hands out of his business area. Chris spent a lot of time going over some of the smallest details with Chuck each day. He would almost be down to ordering office supplies. Chuck didn't know what to do. Chris was his boss, but he was feeling invaded. His own sense of importance and worth in his job had been taken away. He began to feel as though he were incompetent, otherwise Chris would not have to keep telling him what to do. Worse, whenever Chuck did make a decision on his own, Chris would second-guess him, telling him how his decisions were wrong. Finally, Chuck had to make a choice: either quit and get out of this situation, or go through his business life feeling second-rate.

This sort of thing happens so often in business it can qualify as a textbook case study. Managers are very prone to keep intruding in areas where they really have no business. They are often so insecure in their own feelings about their competency that they are afraid to allow anyone who reports to them the freedom to make decisions. Many managers are already caught up in a web of co-dependent thinking and feeling. They are unable to detach themselves from others enough to allow the operation to run smoothly. And when they do intrude on others, they bring the viruses that can cause the same problems in their subordinates.

Once shame finds a foothold, it begins a life of its own. Like most living things, it seeks survival, growth, and perpetuation. As it is nourished, it invades other unsuspecting areas of a person's life. The feelings encountered by such a person in what would ordinarily be a "normal" relationship or transaction also become sources of shame-bound feelings.

This process is one that is enormously destructive since it feeds upon itself. Shame causes unusual interpretations to be placed upon ordinary events, i.e., the person has a shame-bound filtering system through which he tends to see his life. Oftentimes a simple greeting from another person will be examined to see what kind of hidden message is lurking there. These interpretations in turn become sources for more shame-bound feelings, which are continuously added to the reservoir already stored up. Then the accumulated shame finds more means of expression in the affected person's day-to-day life. And so on and on. The shame is not only self-perpetuating, it is constantly growing.

The problem with the process is the person simply does not recognize what is happening to him. The onset is sneaky and the progression insidious. He may have vague feelings all is not right, but his defense mechanisms leap into the breach and assure him everything is just as it is supposed to be. So his very sick behavior becomes normalized in his own thinking. Even though he is presently uncomfortable, he learns to accept it and believe that it is a normal condition of life. Meanwhile the process continues on and on.

CHAPTER 3

BEHAVIORS THAT CREATE AND SUPPORT ORGANIZATIONAL SHAME

The modern business organization has evolved in a particular fashion that presently allows it to create, perpetuate, and exacerbate shame, and thus promote organizational co-dependency. Much of this happens to individuals within the company itself. There are times when we can see characteristics of shame-bound feelings exhibited by the organization itself. Our concern here is with the effect on the individual as well as the resulting effects on the business.

Organizations all develop their unique personalities. To some extent, like humans, each differs from all others. However, there are some points of confluence, places where a number of businesses share common characteristics. Some of these characteristics can have destructive effects on the employees.

We do not believe that businesses intentionally set out to achieve some evil results in dealing with their employees. On the contrary, we believe they have, for the most part, good intentions. How, then, do these unfortunate consequences happen?

Certain systematic dynamics are at work within the organization as it grows and develops. These may be largely unknown to the people in the business itself, relegated to what we would call the unconscious in the human. But they have a tremendous impact on the direction a business will take and how it will interact with its employees. These dynamics occur in groups of any size, whether it be a business, a family, or society as a whole. (We will explore the idea of systems in Chapter 9.)

There are probably many important characteristics we could list. We have selected five to explore here that we think are of particular importance in a business setting. These are: (1) depersonalization, (2) hierarchy, (3) comparisons and competition, (4) poor communication patterns, and (5) lack of appreciation for one's spiritual nature.

To set the background of the modern business organization, we first want to look briefly at some of the history of business in this country, at least from a style-of-management perspective. We believe that the manner in which business in general and management techniques in particular are evolving contribute to the problems we face in this area today.

The business organization as we presently know it is largely a phenomenon of this century. In the early days of this country we were primarily an agrarian society. Most employers had few employees, and often these people were viewed as a part of the employer's extended family. A young person might be apprenticed to a merchant or tradesman. It was common for this apprentice to live with his master's family and really be looked upon as one of that family. The master would provide and care for him in much the same way as he did for his own family. Adult employees usually signed on for life, if not contractually then certainly in practice, never thinking about the mobility we see today in the job market. If this person were to become co-dependent (a term unknown in those times), he would probably develop the personal type we described based upon his contacts with his master and the master's family rather than from his contact with the business per se.

As the country became more urbanized and industrialized in the mid- to late 1800s, we saw the rise of the entrepreneurial manager, the owner-manager who was present and active on the job day by day. This type of manager, even though he had a larger organization to manage, still had a great deal of contact with his employees and often, for better or worse, took on the role of paterfamilias, more or less an extended father-family relationship. This time marked a watershed between an old way of business life and today where it is the hour of the professional manager. In this period there was a gradual weaning of employees from employers, but there was still some interest and sense of social responsibility on the part of the manager-owner about those who worked for him. Here we could have seen a co-dependent created either as a personal type through contacts with people other than the employer, or organizationally through his association with the business.

Today is the age of the professional manager, one who has managerial talents but often has little or no real financial stake in what happens to the business beyond his paycheck and perhaps some stock options or other benefits. In most cases, this management operates at a level totally removed from the workers, usually insulated through several layers of intervening managerial and supervisory personnel. There are basically no interpersonal relationships today between senior management and workers. This developmental process has had a dramatic impact on people in business today, people at all levels in the employment chain, but especially on those who are lower in the table of organization. And so we now look at the effect that has had on business in terms of our topic.

DEPERSONALIZATION

As managers move further away from workers, they become remote figures, often only a name. This very action has created a situation where impersonality reigns. Managers are often seen as figures with great power, people to be feared, respected perhaps, obeyed always. They have become authority figures.

In a large organization, an individual often feels isolated, cut off. He knows that he is in a company but often does not really feel a part of it in a total sense. He is on the payroll, shows up for work each day, does the job, and collects his check. But in matters that really count, especially those having to do with his destiny, he is not a participant. This is particularly interesting since it creates a type of schizophrenic thinking in the employee: he is not really a part of what goes on in the business because he does not make the important decisions; at the same time he often draws much of his own identity and self-assurance from the association. He is somewhat like the kid watching the baseball game through the knothole . . . able to observe, but really not part of the action.

Likewise, there is often little, if any, bonding with fellow employees. They are also just cogs in a very large wheel, other depersonalized units filing in each day to perform their routine tasks. This is largely the assembly line experience. They are rarely seen as friends in the true sense of the word, rather as co-workers. Mutual interests center around company issues during company time, stopping at the company gate.

Employees in big businesses today tend to be largely transitory. Chances are that a co-worker will be transferred to shipping or to Seattle, so it is not really worth much effort to get to know him. Or he may just quit to move to another job.

All of these factors create the vision of a large, impersonal, unfeeling organization, one dedicated to maximum efficiency and profits. It is not seen as having much, if indeed any, concern with the individual worker. Corporate executives are not bad, just busy. They tend to see people in terms of resources, another factor in the equation of profitability. By all means they will talk about the importance of their people at civic luncheons and shareholder meetings, but rarely do they show this level of concern with the employees themselves.

Some of this is natural given the size of many companies. It is not humanly possible for senior managers to reach down through the ranks and know everyone. Where then does this leave the worker? He feels pretty insignificant and unimportant in the overall scheme of things.

We have said that shame-bound, co-dependent people feel bad, inadequate, unworthy, discounted. We strongly believe the impersonality of the large business today feeds directly into these feelings. If the person arrives at the company door a personal co-dependent, business practices are geared to intensify these feelings. If he is particularly susceptible to this problem, the contact with the business creates a place where they can take root and grow.

This is a reality. There is no place to get better reinforcement for feelings of shame outside the family than the modern business setting, unless perhaps one looks at the military, certain churches, and some aspects of government service. This is not just something that happens in passing. It can be a lifetime sentence. If the employee leaves, he'll probably only exchange one organization for a similar one.

The depersonalization fostered in the organization by management tends to spill over and seep down through the ranks. Managers and supervisory personnel below senior management take their cues from their leaders, and when they see the indifference management displays toward workers, they are quick to adopt it as their own. Thus, instead of more personal interaction developing as one moves down through the table of organization, such as might be expected, the tendency towards depersonalization is perpetuated.

Example. We believe one of the best cases that can be made for depersonalization is where the organization develops a system of assigning numbers to employees. The first place this was done in this country on a general and systematic basis was in prisons. There inmates were known as "number so-and-so" rather than by their names. At one time there seemed to be a belief in penology that this type of dehumanizing was somehow merited by the inmates and that this helped in managing them. There is a carry-over on this today, albeit at times for other reasons. It was and is a cruel and unnecessary thing to do. The military picked up on this dehumanizing process, and used it to deal with large numbers of people in a very anonymous fashion, especially in times of war. Later, government found this an advantage in keeping track of records for citizens. So we must now be careful to include our social security number, along with reference, lot, and file numbers in any communications we have with government agencies. Many businesses do this with customers. We now even have impersonal ways of responding through computers that are told what machine responses to give to human requests.

Businesses have fallen into the same trap in the name of efficiency. It becomes easier in a large organization to keep people in place through the use of a payroll number than by name. Before long other employee records began to be maintained in the same way. This reduction of people to numbers is the type of attitude that further promotes depersonalization.

Whether we like it or not, much of what is done with us in our society is dehumanizing in one way or another. To the extent business falls into the same traps it is contributing to the employee's feeling that he is rather insignificant in the total scheme of things. When people begin to have doubts about their own worth, they develop feelings that are ripe for nurturing co-dependent traits. As this continues, the chances of the disease becoming entrenched increase.

HIERARCHY

We have to organize business in some way that makes sense and allows us to accomplish our goals. Corporate structure and strategic planning are important to the survival of a business and go hand in hand. In many large companies the corporate hierarchy tends to become very rigid, almost like an Oriental caste system. There is some upward mobility, but the great majority of employees are more or less stuck. Those who do make the move upward are often those who are well connected, sometimes referred to as the "old boy network" or as people with the "old school tie." Or a person may have a "mentor" or "rabbi" to help him along, someone who has taken another person under his wing and helps guide him along a career path that points toward bigger and better things. Perhaps through a superior education and training he may succeed in his work. (Cermak [1990] has stated that hierarchical systems fit the needs of some co-dependents much more comfortably than do peer relationships.)

But the hierarchical system stifles most people at relatively low levels. It is only occasionally that a person is able to rise rapidly in an organization through sheer hard work, perseverance, and determination. The myth of Horatio Alger, the young man who through diligence and righteous living rises to the top, seems to have taken a permanent vacation in business today. There are again notable exceptions, such as a Lee Iaccoca, who through lots of work, talent, and self-determination has risen to the top. But how many such examples can you find if you search corporate executive suites and boardrooms today?

If a person wants to succeed in a large company, he must first have the indispensable college degree, preferably from some prestigious institution. It does not seem to matter a great deal what the major field of study is once the door has been opened, but the sine qua non for the future executive is more education. We agree that there may be some substance to this approach since the time spent earning a degree usually adds to a person's stability and maturity and makes him appear more reliable. It does, however, foreclose advancement to a large segment of our society today. Being hierarchical is such an integral part of the modern business organization that we rarely think about it at a conscious level. We have come to accept it as a given. It is also by its very nature exclusionary. What actually happens is an allocation of benefits among certain people to the exclusion of others. Anyone who comes from a home or system that supports distance, remoteness, and abandonment will find this type of corporate behavior simply reinforces the notions that he brought to the business with him. And in so doing, it perpetuates a feeling of low self-worth and a sense of aloneness that has been familiar to this person throughout life.

This may seem like an overly dramatic statement to some, yet there is a lot more of this type of feeling around than is observable. People try very hard to mask these feelings and are often successful in doing so, at least to any casual observer. But appearances don't change facts.

This hierarchical system also feeds back into the subject of depersonalization we discussed earlier. We do not know which came first. But they certainly seem to reinforce one another. The separation a hierarchy fosters will just naturally keep management away from employees.

> *Example.* There are all sorts of artificial devices used to separate management from employees. There may be special "perks" for executives: parking places, separate dining rooms, executive washrooms (as though this really made any sense or difference at all), even separate halls and elevators in some really regressive companies. A lot has been said about this sort of thing by writers such as Robert Townsend in *Up the Organization.*

> *Example.* For some reason as we write this, the phrase "Doctor will be with you shortly" keeps coming to mind. Perhaps it is a reminder of the vast importance some people place in titles. We are presently in an academic world where a great deal of time and effort is devoted to the establishment and maintenance of titles. (Some have suggested, perhaps with some basis, that it is higher education's substitute for money.) It is as though the right to use a certain title or rank somehow confers a special status upon the holder to the exclusion of others. If outsiders were able to see this whole process from an inside perspective, they would be amazed. Even as we look around academia and see the basis upon which much of this happens, at times it becomes funny to watch.

COMPARISONS AND COMPETITION

The whole structure of business today is held together by the glue of competition. It seems only natural that companies will compete against one another and that the stronger, absent governmental interference, will survive. The argument can readily be made that consumers benefit from the competitive nature of businesses, that better products become available at fair prices.

What then happens to employees within a company? The co-dependent person, as you'll remember, is one who doesn't have a lot of inner strength. What this means is that he is rather fragile in terms of his own self-concept. So we have him working for a company that is impersonal, is caught up in its own rigid social structure, and now we tell him that he is going to have to compete within that framework. This is a real setup for failure. Remember that he measures failure differently than does a healthy person. What a healthy person can shake off and laugh about becomes a matter of real concern and urgency to the co-dependent. Even things as insignificant as a joke between two people can take on a very harsh meaning to the co-dependent while the "normal" person sees it for what it was intended, laughs, and goes about his business. The co-dependent has a hard enough time coping on a day-to-day basis without the pressures created through a competitive and comparative atmosphere.

We do not mean to imply here that competition should not exist in business. Competition itself is not necessarily bad. In business it is one way that we are able to determine who should move ahead. We are not aiming our comments here at the sort of competition that naturally occurs in organizations, and in life for that matter. Frankly, we do not have a better solution as to how a business will determine who gets promoted, receives more training, etc. What we do object to, and what we think hurts businesses, is the way people within a business interact on a daily basis with one another, and the amount of competitiveness and comparisons occurring there.

Have you ever heard a parent saying to the second or third child, "Why can't you be like your older brother? He always makes straight A's, is captain of the football team, and does everything right"? This is the type of thing we are talking about. We are not talking about the fact that each person will have to rise or fall on his own abilities. But there is a nagging quality to the way many, many supervisors treat their employees.

This is the type of behavior that creates and promotes unhealthy employees. Some people do not have the capacity to tell the other person to get lost. They just sit and take it for hours, days, weeks . . . a lifetime. We stood in a department store in Manhattan (one of "those" stores everyone has heard of) one afternoon and listened to this type of conversation between a supervisor and her employee. The employee had apparently made some mistake, and his supervisor kept nagging him, making the same point over and over again. We finally asked her to quit. When she didn't, we left. Customers do not like to be exposed to internal disputes between employees. In many cases employees do not know they have any choices about this type of treatment. They may feel as though they deserve it. And why not? That is what they have always gotten in life, so it all seems very normal to them. They do not like it, but they have gotten used to it. It simply adds to the "bad" feelings they already have about themselves.

Middle managers can be really cruel at times. When they get on a person's back, they will often tend to stay on him and ride him unmercifully. Others will join in the "fun" because they have seen the pattern set by their supervisor and figure it is okay. Also it may win them some brownie points with the boss. The poor scapegoat will just have to suffer silently. It is his role in life.

> *Example.* We watched an "awards banquet" one time where employ-
> ees were being recognized for their achievements. This is a time-hon-
> ored tradition, and a lot of companies do this regularly. Our criticism
> is not aimed at the idea. But this particular year management had
> intentionally made an effort to honor a few employees in a special
> way to the exclusion of several others. One department had all of its
> people seated at one table. When the awards were handed out, five
> of the people were lavished with praise while three others sat at the
> edge of the spotlight each time it flashed on this table. They had no
> part in the ceremonies and felt left out. Management probably did
> not intend to embarrass these three. However, two of them later said
> they felt very awkward and "ashamed" that they did not get any
> award. They were the "also rans" that evening and felt very left out.
> What was supposed to be a positive evening for everyone turned into
> a nightmare for these two people. They were embarrassed and
> ashamed long after the dinner was over and forgotten.

The whole realm of competitiveness is loaded with the potential for mischief. It takes a very steady hand at the tiller to administer such a program. People who are not too stable cannot be trusted with such responsibility; they do not have the sensitivity to reckon with the feelings of everyone who will possibly be affected.

POOR COMMUNICATION PATTERNS

No study of organizational behavior would be quite complete

without some comments about how an organization communicates. We will have to deal with representative patterns, for we have not focused on one organization. But there are enough similar patterns of poor communications that we can safely generalize.

In a healthy relationship, whether it is with people or organizations, the one point where we might have some hope about maintaining good rapport is through communications with one another. If we are able to communicate openly and freely, without any fear of reprisal, we have a pretty good chance of being able to work out our problems. We can express to one another in a straightforward, nonjudgmental way exactly how we feel at the time, and expect the other person to do the same in return. When our collective souls are on the table, we have some basis for accommodation and change. Can you think of one — just one — organization where this occurs?

Communication patterns in most organizations range from poor to nonexistent. We are going to look at some of the ways *not* to try to communicate. If you find that your organization uses any, some, or all of these, you are in trouble. It means that you have very little communication within the company.

Nonexistent

We can start with the company having no communication. Of course, this is somewhat of an overstatement since all organizations have at least a minimum of intercourse. A minimum level of communication because there are housekeeping and logistical items that have to be taken care of for the company to continue to exist, especially, for example, when figures or numerical data have to be reported. What we are looking at specifically is any type of communication among company members beyond this. Now you might think that this is an exaggeration, but do not dismiss it so lightly. There are in fact a large number of organizations today, especially smaller ones, where this is precisely what is going on.

To the obvious question of "why?" there are a variety of answers. Probably most commonly management does not have any consideration for or trust in its employees. It figures that these people are getting enough if they put in a day's work and draw their pay. Such a cavalier attitude, thank goodness, is rapidly disappearing. There are, however, some holdouts.

This attitude reflects the worst that management has to offer its employees. It completes the circle of isolation that so many employees already feel. It is a loud statement about the indifference of managers toward the people who work for them. It feeds into a lot of the behaviors and feelings we have been discussing.

One-Way Communication

Some companies thrive on communications that only travel one way. This can be in any direction, but normally it will be from the top down. This represents one step above the case where no communication takes place. What management seems to be saying here is that we are willing to share a certain amount of information with you, but we really do not care whether you have any feelings or reactions to what we are telling you. We neither expect nor want any input from you. This type of indifference in some ways is worse than no communication since the employees now have some insight into what is going on but are not supposed to say anything about it. It is like someone has told you something really important and then will not allow you to voice your feelings. It is often hard to hold feelings in at this point, and sometimes they come out in ways that are destructive to the relationship, such as when an employee blows up and acts inappropriately by telling the boss off.

Answer Expectancy

In this case the pattern of communication is such that management anticipates and programs the answers it wants. This is usually so transparent it would seem funny and childish if it were not being used to operate businesses.

The message in this case is that management is willing to give employees some degree of input yet is uncomfortable with anything other than programmed responses. So it constructs a situation where there is an illusion of participative management, something the CEO has heard from a speaker at a conference or read about in a magazine, and allows the employees to be part of the plan. The whole thing is farcical because there is no way the employees will really have a vote. It is a waste of work hours, and management would be better off just making the decision itself and announcing it to the workers.

Example. We saw an excellent example a few years ago that neatly illustrates this. A large company was doing space planning for a new building it was erecting. There were five floor plans presented to various employees' groups that showed different ways the new building could be laid out. Management had already been sold on a specific design by its architects (an open office system, one which made almost no sense to anyone below senior management.) Plan 1 had been previously rejected out of hand by management. Plan 5 was so ridiculous that no one would accept it. Plans 2 and 4 were variations of 1 and 5 and would obviously be unacceptable. So this left Plan 3, which is what management wanted and had programed all along. This situation was a rather transparent one, but it actually happened. The answer had been carefully programed so that management could get what it wanted while workers were supposed to feel that they had a hand in the decision. One vice-president challenged the architects but was shut down very quickly by one of his superiors. (The plan, incidentally, caused a lot of problems over the years to come, both for employees and for customers.)

For workers who have any sense at all, this type of exercise is more insulting than if management had simply taken a position and announced it to employees. It looks like someone does not think workers are very bright, and this generally makes people extremely angry.

Indirect

The next type of communication is what we call indirect. This can occur in a number of ways but commonly will fall into one of two categories. The first type is gossip. This is where a supervisor tries to communicate with employees by dropping some gossip with other employees in the hope, and often assurance, that it will work its way back to the targeted employee. And oftentimes this is what will happen. This allows the supervisor to get the information disseminated without having a distasteful confrontation with the employee.

Example. We saw a situation in one organization where the boss made it a habit to take one employee aside each day and talk to her about the others who were working there. This put the employee in a terrible fix: she did not want to be disloyal to her employer, but in a way she wanted to tell her co-workers what the boss thought of their work so they could have a chance to correct it. She played this game for a while until she began to realize what was happening. She then refused to be the conduit anymore. Her boss soon dropped his personal, intimate conversations with her and turned to another employee to become the carrier of information.

The second type is similar but does not have the wide circulation. In this case the supervisor will tell another employee something he wants communicated with some type of indication that the word is to be passed along to the targeted employee. Again, he has avoided any direct communication while still getting the word out.

> *Example.* This type of communication is most often delivered hierarchically. For example, we saw one company where the CEO generally refused to talk to anyone except the executive vice-president. He would pass information along, which that officer was then expected to tell other employees, usually executives. There was, however, an interesting but common twist to this. When the information was good, the CEO took it upon himself to be the bearer of the news. If it was bad, his hatchet man got the job.

Memos

One of the worst days that ever happened in business was when someone discovered he could communicate with his employees through memos. A memo is one of the most impersonal types of communication and is misused and abused by a majority of managers. It allows for anonymous communication. It can be used to inform, intimidate, and harass employees and protects the manager from any personal interaction. Many times memos are simply used to cover the writer in case something goes wrong later, commonly known as CYA (cover your ass).

All these types of communications are characteristics of a business that does not have much regard or respect for its employees. It may be that the managers themselves are caught up in some type of addictive behavior and simply do not know how to interact with their employees. Or it may be that this has been historically the way things have been done in this organization and no one has the strength to stand up and suggest that it be done differently. Perhaps the managers are just indifferent to the needs and concerns of employees.

> *Example.* We knew the chairman of a large utility company in the Southwest a few years ago who scorned memos. He told us one day,

"Never write anything down. Someday five years from now some silly SOB will come waving it in your face." This manager would accept memos but would confine his responses to "Yes," "No," or "See me" written in one corner. He did not write memos. He thought they wasted a lot of time and money, especially since most of his employees worked in one place and had telephones to call and feet to walk to another office to talk in person.

Memos may have some limited uses. Some messages in far-flung operations have to be communicated, and some type of writing is needed. But most of the time they are simply expedient ways to avoid direct communication.

Example. We saw another organization where the CEO had a real love affair with memos. It would be hard to estimate the number he generated each day. He had three portable dictating machines and was quite literally never without one. He roamed around the business, sometimes on weekends, constantly speaking into his machine. Another extremely irritating habit he had was his style. Memos often began with "I was disappointed today to see . . . ," "It was my understanding that you were going to . . . ," "Perhaps I was mistaken, but. . . . " The irony in this was that he really felt this was a gentle, thoughtful, and effective way of dealing with employees. They, however, were enraged by his missives. This was one of the most blatant examples of memo misuse we have seen and one that was very destructive to the internal harmony of the organization.

LACK OF APPRECIATION FOR ONE'S SPIRITUAL NATURE

We hesitated for a long while before deciding to include this section; there is a lot of negative reaction to discussions of this sort in a business setting. We included it for three reasons. First, we decided the book would be incomplete without it. Second, we are concerned because there is often so little positive regard in business today for an individual's spiritual nature. Finally, we believe spirituality is one of the foundation stones for recovery from co-dependence.

Businesses often tend to romp roughshod over employee values and beliefs. They largely ignore what people hold as being ultimately important for the ways they live their lives. This, in turn, results in a lot of inner turmoil and conflict among employees about their own sense of identity and value within an organization, and about the true identity and value of the organization itself.

We believe that humans are spiritual animals. That is not something we are prepared to defend: you will either accept it or reject it. Many people have a knee-jerk reaction when they hear the term "spiritual" or "spirituality," equating it to "religion." This is too bad. For better or worse, and for whatever reasons, a lot of adults in today's world have a negative reaction to organized religion. This is often due to childhood exposure through well-meaning parents and other adults who force-fed their kids with a brand of harsh, anti-intellectual dogma that those kids, now grown up, find they can no longer accept. Or it may be the result of no exposure at all. Or perhaps God (or some Higher Power) has "failed" that person, and he can no longer accept the whole idea.

We believe that there is a vast difference between spirituality and religion. They may intersect at times, and often do, but may exist independently of one another. Religion has to do with some type of organized form of worship, usually accompanied by rituals, dogma, specific forms, buildings, and a hierarchy. Spirituality, on the other hand, is an individual matter, and has to do with how a person lives his life in a way that makes some type of sense in this world.

Bernie Siegel, in his excellent book *Love, Medicine, and Miracles,* has said that "Spirituality means the ability to find peace and happiness in an imperfect world, and to feel that one's own personality is imperfect. From this peaceful state of mind come both creativity and the ability to love unselfishly, which go hand in hand. Acceptance, faith, forgiveness, peace and love are the traits that define spirituality for me" (1986).

Co-dependency may be seen as a sickness of the soul. People who suffer from it, like most other addictions, are in a spiritual crisis. (For an excellent discussion of spirituality in addiction and recovery see Vernon Johnson's *I'll Quit Tomorrow*, 1980.) For the co-dependent, the one who is largely without some firm foundation upon which to rest his life, this lack of respect for the individual simply fans the fires of negative feelings and discontent. He feels as though he has been overlooked, neglected, and perhaps even abused by the organization that at the same time is demanding his loyalty. It adds one more stick on an already overburdened back.

We believe that if there were but one effort that business could make that would help alleviate the problems of co-dependents in business, it would be to recognize and loudly proclaim the unique value of the individual and his ability to contribute to the organization. By contributing we mean that each person could make his own particular type of contribution in a way that had meaning to him.

We feel that problems with the spiritual nature of man fall into some general categories that we can identify and discuss. We will look at three of these: (1) problems that deal with ethical issues or breaches of faith between the employer and employee, (2) situations where there is an invasion of the individual's privacy, and (3) issues surrounding inconsistencies and a lack of empathy with organizational behavior in terms of the how the individual is treated.

We recently observed a situation in one organization that addresses both an ethical and breach of faith issue.

> **Example.** In the organization we observed there was a more or less structured policy for promotion. That is, if a person did certain things, the written policy said he could be promoted to the next grade. Unknown to many, the senior executive in this division had an unwritten policy. He believed that a person should fulfill certain other requirements in some cases. The problem was that this had neither been communicated to the people who worked for him nor committed to writing for all to see. Promotions were reviewed once a year and selections made at that time. Criteria seemed to vary from year to year without any discernible pattern. With some people who had completed all of the paper requirements, promotions were granted, while with others it was denied based upon the unwritten beliefs of the division head. It was much like a football player's plunging for a touchdown only to find the goal line had been moved back another ten yards. This was challenged by some employees as being not only a possible legal breach of contract, but certainly a lack of good faith and ethics. The division head responded with silence, the last retreat of someone who has little regard for the spiritual nature of those who work for him and an uncertain ethical basis for his decision.

This "public be damned" attitude, fortunately, is on the wane. However, there are still managers who deal in an arbitrary decision-making that has far-reaching and profound effects on the lives of those who work for them. When a manager does not keep faith with his employees, he engages in a type of behavior that destroys confidence and respect. The confidence and respect denied to the employees are then denied to the manager. This condition soon promotes a lot of problems within an organization.

Great controversy has arisen over the past decade about precisely how much right an employer has to inquire into the private lives of employees and job applicants. This has especially been highlighted through the use of drug testing, lie detector tests, and psychological testing. We recently heard about another situation that illustrates this from another vantage point.

> *Example.* In this organization there are about forty employees. The boss has a rule whereby he goes through each piece of mail received at the office each day and reads it before he gives it to the employee to whom it is addressed. (There may be an interesting footnote about the legality of such an act under current postal laws.) We know that this happens in businesses such as stock brokerages as matter of internal audit control so that management can know what orders have been executed and to be able to see money as it comes into the firm. There seems to be little doubt that this is a good procedure and one that is necessary to fulfill their fiduciary duties to customers. However, this particular company is not in a business where there is that type of sensitivity. If the boss is out of the office, the employee may ask his secretary and get permission to see the mail, but cannot remove it until the boss has had an opportunity to review it. We do not know what the rationale is for a protocol such as this, but see it as being very intrusive on the privacy of the individual employee.

There can be no reasonable justification for management's invading the privacy of its employees unless there is some overriding public issue at stake, for example, public safety. It is almost akin to some prurient interest in the lives of employees, which has nothing to do with the operation of the business.

Inconsistencies and lack of empathy both by organizations and within them can cause tremendous harm to individuals and in some cases cause irreparable damage.

Example. The examples we give throughout this book are riddled with inconsistencies. It is one of the enduring characteristics in co-dependent people, the common thread weaving through all actions. We want to focus on one case example that illustrates this problem in the context under discussion.

Joe was a senior executive in his company. He saw himself as a hands-on type of manager, i.e., he was very involved in a lot of the details in his particular division. He felt this helped his employees while giving him a sense of control. Actually, Joe was more what we would call a dabbler. He would go into an area, spend some time there, raise questions and issues, and give advice. It would look like he was really going to focus on this particular problem. Then he would disappear. Often he would reach down through the organizational structure, bypassing intermediate managers in his eagerness to isolate and look at a specific problem. Joe saw all of this as part of his job and of being helpful. After a while others saw it as a nuisance, an intrusion. After Joe disappeared, there was a great deal of confusion. Nobody really knew where to turn or what to do. Managerial authority had been undermined since Joe had worked around them. The final chapter, however, was not written at that point. After he had intruded and created chaos, Joe was often angry and critical when the problem did not get solved his way and on his timetable. Middle managers were caught in between. They did not know what Joe actually wanted since he had not communicated with them, but they were held accountable nevertheless. By using this type of inconsistent management-by-confusion, Joe stripped his managers of much of their self-worth and feelings of usefulness. He had no regard for what happened to these people inside.

We have seen a lot of Joes. They are active at all levels in businesses in nearly any organization one observes. They have little regard for the inner feelings and worth of those who work for them. They often mean well, but lack any real empathy. The result is spiritual damage to the employees.

CHAPTER 4

SHAME

An interesting study for someone in the future might be to determine how over the past 100 years or so we could possibly have neglected the role that shame plays in our lives. It has eluded the most creative, original, and insightful minds that have explored the human psyche over the past century. And yet, as we are now learning, shame may well be at the center of many, if not most, of our addictions, mental disorders, and problems in interpersonal relationships. John Bradshaw has explored this idea more thoroughly in his recent book *Bradshaw On: Healing the Shame That Binds You* (1988), in which he places shame at the heart of most mental disorders.

Gershen Kaufman started writing about shame in 1972, and other authors and researchers such as Fossum and Mason, as well as Bradshaw, have enlarged upon the concept in the past three to four years. So most of our knowledge comes from relatively recent work, and we are just now beginning to gain insights into this dynamic.

There has been a tendency for many years to place guilt and shame under one heading and to use the two terms synonymously. It is true that there are many overlaps in how these two problems manifest themselves, and it is equally true that the dynamics of these two often intersect. So it is sometimes hard to neatly segregate shame from guilt, at least based upon observable behavior.

And yet, these represent two separate and distinct problems when dealing with troubled people. Guilt is the more simple and more healthy of the two, one that tends to have a reasonable origin, a predictable course, a treatable pattern, and a satisfactory conclusion. Shame, on the other hand, is grounded in unreasonableness, takes on all kinds of different forms, tends to elude treatment, and usually is not resolved. (Some may argue that guilt sometimes is also "unreasonable," and we will concede that this is true. The point here is that shame always bears the "unreasonableness" quality, while guilt is often appropriate to the event causing it.)

Guilt is fairly simple. It is the feeling that a person has when a rule has been broken — some norm violated. Society or the environment may have imposed these rules, or they may have been developed internally as a part of one's belief system. Many rules come from one's family and religion. Such rules are commonly known and respected, and all or most people agree in the social compact to be guided and governed by such rules.

When a person transgresses a rule, he feels guilt. We can sometimes identify this feeling as one of remorse. It is the feeling that "I've done something bad, or wrong." We all understand that rules need to be obeyed, and we disappoint ourselves when we disobey them. Quite often penalties or sanctions await the person who violates them. Society then demands that the punishment should fit the crime.

So, what do we have? We have an agreed-upon rule that is clear in its meaning and appropriate punishment awaiting offenders. When a person steps over the line, the feelings he experiences are proportionate to the infraction. Thus, a person would feel much worse after killing another human than if he had merely hit him, and the punishment in the former case would be more severe. This distinction is important to note because, as we shall see, shame is very different.

Since the price the offender pays is also proportionate to the offense, once the penalty is paid, the price extracted, the feelings of guilt can be expiated, and the offender is free to proceed with his life without this additional baggage. People are often able to work through guilt feelings on their own, although sometimes it will require professional help. The important thing is that throughout, guilt has a reasonable and rational quality to it. It is grounded in reality. It makes good sense to a majority of people.

What, then, happens to the person who is shame-bound? If we were to take the important elements of guilt and ascribe "reasonableness" to them, to describe shame we would have to start with the idea of "unreasonableness." Almost everything about shame defies logic and reason. It arises not out of a transgression of a rule that makes sense, but rather from some perceived deficiency the actor believes he sees in his own character. While guilt is essentially outward directed, shame is almost wholly internal. Shame usually does not arise from a single act; it generally comes from an inner feeling of helplessness and hopelessness that develops over time.

The events collectively leading to feelings of shame have nothing to do with the real world. Those events are generally totally disproportionate to the feelings and problems they create. While guilt says "I have done something bad," shame says "I am bad." Once a person is stripped of his essential goodness, he feels lost and without hope of redemption.

Shame is not a passing feeling of remorse. It becomes a personality characteristic, one which permeates and infects all other aspects of one's personality, affecting or shading all thoughts, perceptions, and behaviors. It is a sickness of the soul. A "bad person" has a lot of trouble believing he is good or that he can do good things or that good things will happen to him.

Since shame affects the person in such a global sense, it is difficult to isolate and treat. It has an almost universal application in the affected person's life. It may manifest itself as one or more of many abnormal or aberrational patterns of thought or behavior. Quite often in therapy, the client, as well as the professional, go off chasing symptoms, but never really confront and treat the problem. And so, predictably, as one symptom is treated successfully, another mysteriously appears to cause mischief or destruction. Treatment is never really concluded; there just seems to be a lifetime full of crises and problems to be dealt with.

Shame has become a way of life for many people. This is terribly sad because it will probably be misdiagnosed and improperly treated. And finally, the affected person will simply give up and become resigned to a life full of pain and maladjustive behavior. The saddest part of all is to see the waste of human beings who could be helped.

Example. We use a simple example to distinguish between guilt and shame. First, imagine you are driving down the street and get pulled over for speeding. You were going ten miles over the speed limit. You have broken a rule and now must pay the penalty. You may feel a little remorse, guilt, but it soon goes away. You pay the fine and go along your way.

Second, imagine that you are a ballplayer and you have worked hard all year, gone to all the practices, done everything you could, in the hope that you will get to play. But the season finally ends, and you never got into the game. You were not good enough. That is how the shame-bound person feels, never quite good enough to play.

Shame can be classified according to where it occurs in time in the following ways: (1) new, (2) inherited, (3) multigenerational, (4) maintained, and (5) dormant.

New shame is that which we only recently encountered, something which has not been with us for a long time nor in our families or associates in the past. It is something we have just experienced and which, for some reason, we have not been equipped to deal with effectively.

Inherited shame is something that we acquire from someone else, usually a family member or someone significant enough in our lives to be very close to us. This type of shame may be unspoken, and we can acquire it largely through osmosis. This may be something that began as a pretty unimportant event but has assumed much larger proportions over time.

Multigenerational shame spans two or more generations. It most commonly occurs in a family but may also be found in a business. It is the family secret, that item too big to talk about but which everyone, at least in previous generations, knows about. The insidious part of this type is that members of a future generation may have the same experiences but be unable to determine the real source of the problem. This information is normally only available from ancestors, and if they die without passing along the information, it is lost to their survivors.

Maintained shame is a nagging type, which is constantly with a person and which both feeds into and is fed by daily events in a person's life. It may wax and wane in its effects, but it's always more or less present.

Dormant shame is the type that is still with a person but has gone into a holding pattern for some reason. Perhaps it was not really very strong in the beginning and there have been no events sufficiently strong or on point that could resurrect it. It lies there silently, waiting for some particular event that will allow it to emerge from its present state into an active force in the person's life.

We can find each of these varieties of shame present in both personal and organizational co-dependency. Once an organization becomes infected with inherited or multi-generational shame, the shame tends to be self-perpetuating and is passed from generation to generation. As in families, after the passage of time its members are not even aware that shame is actively present, much less able to identify its source. This situation is especially problematic since an organization is not going to be able to combat something it cannot even identify. Its members will know something is wrong but will have no idea what it is or why it is there.

CHAPTER 5

SHAME-BASED BEHAVIORS

The idea of co-dependency has been explored over the past decade by a number of writers. They have done a pretty thorough job of looking at the dynamics, and, while this job is not complete, the purpose of this book is not to repeat a lot of what has already been done. It does seem appropriate, however, to briefly discuss co-dependency, to define it as we understand it, and to show how we believe it applies to business.

We have previously defined co-dependency as the condition where a person tries to control another and be responsible for the consequences of the behavior of that person. Writers vary greatly on the prevalence of co-dependency in this country. Hafen has suggested that at least forty million people alone are affected by chemically dependent persons, while others have placed the number of people who are co-dependent at one time or another as high as 98 percent of the population. Whatever yardstick you use to measure the extent of the problem, a very significant part of our population is in fact caught in this web, and a lot of those people work every day. When we see the extent of the problem, we believe that the more businesses and employees know about this whole area, the better equipped they will be to avoid some of the pitfalls that plague victims.

If so many people are affected by co-dependency, has it become statistically "normal"? That is certainly a fair question, but one we are not certain can be answered with any real accuracy. The best that probably can be said is that even if such a case could be made, it does not make pathological (diseased) co-dependent behavior any more healthy. "Normal" does not necessarily imply "healthy."

Why does one person have so many more problems with this than does another? Like most other addictive behaviors, co-dependency affects different people in different ways. If we take the most extreme case and assume that in fact most of us have co-dependent characteristics at times, and if we assume that co-dependency really can be debilitating, why are more of us not really sick? Our opinion is that probably everyone has some of the symptoms of co-dependency at some time. Some people stay caught up in the problem while others are able to move through that situation and come out the other end relatively unscathed, and perhaps wiser for the experience. Those who do not move on run the risk of developing pathological problems.

Co-dependency, no matter what its origins, has a number of common characteristics. Here we want to look briefly at some characteristic behavior patterns. It is important to note at the outset that co-dependency is no respecter of sex, age, status, or any other true or artificial classification. We all are potential victims. As we discuss examples, we will use both male and female actors. There is nothing implied in this other than an effort to avoid the pitfalls of sexism.

PLACING OTHERS BEFORE SELF

The co-dependent person almost always places the wants and needs of others, either people or organizations, before her own. She feels a sense of obligation to others, which translates into excessive loyalty. She will see herself as a good person, one who is genuinely caring. To some extent this may be true. However, when her own needs continue to be unfulfilled day after day, on and on, something is very wrong.

> *Example.* Mary is an example of a person who displays the sacrificial type of behavior we are discussing. She worked for a group of professionals as office manager. As the years went by, she assumed more and more responsibilities. Sometimes people would not want to do or have the time to do certain things, and she would take on their responsibilities. She felt like the job simply had to get done, and so she did it, even though it meant a lot of extra hours working at night. After she had been there about fifteen years, she took a look at her own life and realized that it was empty. She was unable to have relationships with others because she did not have time or the energy to do anything but work. It was difficult to have intimate relationships

with men because she was never available. As she experienced the loneliness and depression of her life, she finally sought help. Mary was addicted as surely as someone who takes drugs or drinks alcohol. She was addicted to her work and the amount of control she felt she exerted daily in the office. She had become co-dependent to the job.

Are there really saints, people who are truly good and who give to others? Sure, we think so. If so, how can they be distinguished from co-dependents? People do good things for others, and that is to be prized and commended. The dividing line might be described in this way: if the person goes to bed every night angry because she spent so much time on others that she did not get her own things done that day, she has got a problem. The motivation of saints is different also. They tend to do good works for their own sake; co-dependents do "good deeds" to gain some control over another person or thing. (Cermak speaks about "healthy" co-dependency, the point at which a person has not taken on pathological characteristics that interfere with other parts of her life.)

LOSS OF IDENTITY

As time goes on, the co-dependent begins to lose her sense of personal identity. She becomes more absorbed in the other person and will tend to draw her own self-worth and sense of being from what happens in that other person's life. Basically, if the targeted person is okay, she is okay; if he is not, she is a mess. There is such a total emotional, physical, and spiritual commitment to the other person that the co-dependent does not have time to establish her own identity.

With this comes a loss of what is referred to as boundaries. There is no definable structure that clearly delineates and establishes the roles of people who become co-dependents. Distinctions become blurred, and the co-dependent is nearly completely immersed in the personality of another. She will see intimacy as physical closeness and deep concern for the well-being of the other person. And while these are factors in healthy, intimate behavior, the co-dependent will become compulsive in these two areas. In couples counseling there is often an unhealthy partner who becomes enmeshed with the other, healthy partner. A healthy person will resist attempts to overrun his identity boundaries and will want his own space. The co-dependent will interpret this as rejection and will cling more tightly to her partner. The result is that one partner is always pursuing aggressively while the other is always running away. Ultimately, there is usually a breakup where the un-healthy partner is left devastated, very confused, and depressed. She will be unable to figure out what happened and will interpret that as just more evidence that she is not okay.

> *Example.* When we interviewed Karen and we asked her to tell us something about herself, all she talked about was her job and the work she performed. As we tried to guide her in other directions, she constantly returned to work. It had become for her the only way in which she could describe herself. Her whole identity was wrapped up in what she did occupationally. This is not too surprising when we consider that she did very little else with her life.
>
> Karen had truly lost her own identity. She could not define herself in any way other than through her work. The boundaries between what she was like as a person and her work persona had blurred to a point where they were inseparable. An additional problem arises when a person like Karen finally has to retire. She is left quite literally without a personality.

UNSTABLE EMOTIONS

The co-dependent will make a valiant effort to control her own emotions. She will adopt one of two contrasting behavioral patterns: (1) she will try to control her feelings by shutting down emotionally in the belief that if no one can see how she really feels then the problems do not exist; or (2) she will believe that she must express every feeling she has, thus resorting to overdramatizing life's events, sometimes to the point of hysteria.

Obviously, these behaviors are unhealthy for the person and both confusing and uncomfortable for others. They do not really represent what is going on inside the person, but rather are artificial forms of behavior that she feels will protect her.

Another technique favored by the co-dependent is acting out. When she is faced with the prospect of losing her partner, or even when she feels that she is not getting enough attention (seen by her as rejection), she simply has a "fit," i.e., she throws a tantrum. This can take place in many different forms ranging from crying and screaming to becoming actually physically ill or mentally impaired temporarily.

At times it is as though she has gone temporarily insane.

She gets the attention she wants in perhaps the only way she knows how to ask for it. Everyone is focused on her. When she is through, she has said and done things she would not normally say and do. It is as though a little child inside her jumped out for a while, had a temper tantrum, attacked others, and then retreated to the safety inside. She may feel some remorse for a time, but otherwise she feels relieved because she got her much-needed attention. What a sad thing that she does not know that she has choices, other ways to satisfy her needs.

On the other hand, those around her have reacted to her in their own ways, which may include co-dependency of their own, and are often left in a state of turmoil and with a lot of anger and unresolved feelings. They are often confused about what has just happened and may feel threatened in the relationship. Lots of times these people will carry around the aftermath of this blowup for several days.

> *Example.* Helen was a lovely person. She was the type of person anyone would like to have for a friend. She was happy, outgoing, had a serious side, attentive, caring . . . all of the good qualities a person could ask for. Helen also had an ugly side. Very few people saw this, mostly only those in her immediate family. Helen would go along fine for several weeks, or even months, and then would go into a rage (or tantrum) that would shock others and astonish herself. It would seem to come out of nowhere. There were no real triggers she could identify, and when it happened, it was usually over something insignificant. Helen would rage, scream, swear, and treat those about her in a terrible way. They would look on, not knowing what to do. When it subsided, usually in about an hour, she would feel deep remorse. Helen could not figure out what was happening to her. At times she felt like she was going crazy. What she was to learn was that this was "normal" behavior for a co-dependent. When a co-dependent person does not get her needs met, when she does not get the attention she feels she deserves, she will often create a real crisis. By doing this, she gets everyone to focus on her; so she finally receives the attention, albeit negative, she has been seeking. She feels terrible for a while, but later she feels okay, since the tantrum gave her what she wanted.

This is particularly damaging in a business setting. Many managers will see this type of behavior as unacceptable. When it occurs in a supervisory person, the effect is immeasurable. It is almost the same as when a child experiences a parent out of control, one of the most frightening experiences a child can have.

COMPULSIVE BEHAVIOR

The co-dependent person is caught up in an addictive cycle characterized by compulsive behavior. The primary addiction is the need to be totally involved with another person. However, if the compulsions he feels are frustrated, he may shift his needs to some other area. For example, we often see co-dependents becoming chemically dependent, workaholics, overeaters, etc. The dynamics of addiction are already firmly rooted, and it then becomes a matter of simply shifting compulsions from a person to some object or substance. The goal of this compulsive behavior is the attempt by the co-dependent to find some person, object, or event that, in his mind, will help him feel better about himself. The belief is that if he can only attain what he is seeking, everything will be fine. Of course, that never happens. One of the terrible consequences stemming from this type of behavior is the illusion, and sometimes the actual feeling, that the person is better. This is part of the insidious nature of addictions generally. It prompts the person to seek more of the same behavior in the belief that it will somehow cure him. Thus, the addictive process tends to be self-perpetuating.

The fallacy lies in the fact that by turning to things or people external to himself he can never truly develop his own sense of self-worth or find any lasting relief from the shame-bound feelings that plague him. The solutions to these problems lie within the person, meaning that there must be a substantial change internally, not externally, to find peace of mind and comfort.

> *Example*. Tom is a real person, although he is representative of many, many others who have lived the same way. Tom had been through treatment for alcoholism. When he came out and went back to his family, he found that all of a sudden he had a lot of extra time on his hands. He began to fill some of this time by attending meetings of Alcoholics Anonymous twice a day. After a while this was not enough. So he began taking courses toward a masters degree. He did not do this the normal way by taking one, or perhaps two, courses each term. He took a minimum of three courses each semester. His work filled up every day, and the school filled up most evenings.

Weekends were devoted to studying. In between he still attended A.A. meetings. When he filled every minute of every day, it caused some real conflict in his relationships with his family. They had expected to have some claim to his time when he started recovery, but what they found out was that he simply substituted work and school for his old drinking compulsions.

When the co-dependent does go into recovery, he will need to reach out to others and try to find new networks that will support him in the new direction his life is taking. As he does this, he may at times revert to old behavior and become clinging again. His partner may have an equally difficult time in playing her part. She may not particularly like the old life, but it had become familiar. And there is a well-defined human tendency to resist changing the known and familiar.

HYPERVIGILANCE

The co-dependent person has especially sensitive antennae. In fact, she can sometimes see or sense things that no one else in the world notices — almost as if they really are not there. She feels that she has to keep a constant watch on her particular partner in order to anticipate his needs and moods. If she believes that something in his life is going wrong, or is about to, she needs to move quickly to prevent this from happening. Or if it has already happened, she has got to get it straightened out right away so everything will be okay again. This constant watching requires a lot of energy. It detracts from the co-dependent's taking care of herself.

Example. When Alice came in the office each morning, the first thing she did was to check out her supervisor, Mike. Mike was a mecurical person, and no one ever could predict what he was going to be like as the new day started. Alice was especially sensitive to this. When Mike was in a bad mood, she tried to cheer him up. When he felt okay, she tried to find little ways throughout the day to keep him that way. Alice was very attentive to Mike's mood swings. If he began to drift, she would try to rescue him. Maybe taking some reports to him ahead of time would make him happy. Or perhaps she should stay out of the way. Maybe if she was especially cheerful, Mike would feel better. Alice invested a lot of her energy each day into these tasks.

Example. Another interesting example we saw in one organization was the behavior of management-level executives. The president of this company was a person who had strange working hours, coming in very early some days, staying late others, not even showing up on some. Even stranger, he had some expectations that his executives would be there when he was. These people were so attuned to this that they would creep down the hall before leaving in the evening to see if the president was still in his office. If he was still working, they would quietly return to their own offices and continue to work until the president had finally left — strange behavior for a group of highly priced, mature executives. They were, however, so attuned to the boss that they were afraid to go home at something approximating a normal quitting time.

MOOD SWINGS

The co-dependent person will generally have wide mood swings. One reason is that at any given time her feelings are keyed to another person. Importantly, it does not really matter how that other person really feels, but how the co-dependent perceives and believes he feels. So her partner may just simply feel like being quiet for a while, having a little time to himself. The co-dependent can view this as something being wrong, a feeling she will translate into "I've done something wrong or he'd talk to me." These mood swings will range from major depression to the euphoric bordering on manic, and everything and place in between. She will ride the roller coaster up and down daily based upon what she thinks she sees. This often makes the individual feel as though she is going crazy.

Because she does not ever really know what the day will bring, she waits in a more or less constant state of anxiety. She wants everything to work but is constantly afraid that something will happen or it will not. The anxiety she feels tends to exaggerate the mood swings. She will take insignificant things and blow them up into something gigantic. Conversely, she will tend to skip lightly over areas in her life that are truly important. It is as though she has a set of binoculars and always seems to look through the wrong end — magnifying little things and minimizing large ones.

Example. Jan was a classic co-dependent. We knew that within a short time after meeting her. Her moods varied with what was happening in her work as well as in her personal life. For example, one day when her boss casually commented that she looked like she had put on a couple of pounds, Jan went into a state of frantic depression, feeling that she looked awful. The comment made her feel generally inadequate. She was still depressed when she got home that night. This affected everyone in her family. In Jan's case, her husband, Ted, was also co-dependent and had his own set of problems. As Jan's moods swung up and down, so did Ted's. He believed he should be responsible for how she felt, and that if she were feeling bad, he should do something to make her feel better. As they both went through these changes, their children experienced the inconsistencies that come from living in an addictive home. They were affected as surely as if one or both of their parents had been chemically dependent. This is an excellent example of how co-dependency in a business setting creates a ripple effect that reaches further into a person's life than simply what has happened on the job.

VICTIMS OF ABUSE

The majority of co-dependents are victims of some type of abuse. It may not be verbal, physical, or sexual, but can often be emotional or psychological. While these five may be different in their applications, they all feed into the co-dependent's self-image of shame-bound feelings — "I got what I deserved" or "He wouldn't have done that if I hadn't. . . . " Abuse of any kind is the worst act, short of homicide, one human can inflict upon another. It is enormously destructive to both the abuser and the victim.

People who are healthy have a hard time imagining and understanding abusive behavior. They do not see why anyone would stay in an abusive relationship. The problem is that they do not understand co-dependent thinking. Co-dependents just do not know that they have choices. They believe they are stuck wherever they happen to be.

Example. In one company we saw, the president had this abusive habit of speaking through others. For example, if he wanted A to get some message, he would tell B, knowing that B would pass the word along. He had one person, Randy, who was a favorite target for some of this treatment. Randy had been with the company for about ten years and was a well-paid executive. He was also a person who was not too certain of himself, at least with respect to his president. The president would frequently tell B that he did not know whether

Randy was going to be able to keep his job, or sometimes he would say he was thinking about firing Randy. B would dutifully pass this on to Randy, who would become very anxious and scared. If Randy tried to talk to the president about this, he would be assured that everything was fine. And so Randy spent most of his work life in real confusion. The president, incidentally, was an alcoholic, and Randy was a classic business co-dependent.

ANXIETY

Anxiety itself is not bad. It is a human condition. Existentialists believe that, if we had no anxiety, we probably would not get much done. It seems to be a force that turns our attention in one direction or another and spurs us on to try to achieve something.

Anxiety is the constant, uncomfortable feeling that something bad is going to happen. The sources of stress have to be separated between what is real and what is merely imagined. When the source is real, the anxiety it provokes is caused by some event that has happened, is happening, or is about to happen. Such feelings then come from the expectations the individual has about the probable outcomes of such an event. Now this type of situation does in fact deal with reality and should be encountered head-on by any person. Typically, the co-dependent person will often try to avoid dealing with this. He will pretend that whatever the problem is does not exist. Or he takes the problem and begins to look at it out of its context in such a way that it becomes much bigger or very different than it actually is. Each case is a technique that the co-dependent will use to avoid having to deal with the reality of the situation. Remember that co-dependents by definition do not relate well to the real world.

It has been suggested that there are two other types of anxiety besides the real one. Freud called the second one neurotic anxiety since it stems from events or situations that are not real or that are so vague that they cannot be defined. His third one is labeled moral anxiety and occurs when the person's response to events in his life conflict with his value system.

In looking at these, one can see that so-called neurotic anxiety is bread and butter to the co-dependent. It again represents a world that does not exist and transports him away from reality. He can then allow his magical mind to conjure up all sorts of situations, dealing largely with "what ifs."

It is a projection into the future where the person looks at outcomes. The problem, of course, is that most of the time there is no problem.

Moral anxiety for a healthy person exists when he has a conflict between his values and what he perceives as the direction his life is taking. He faces a type of moral crisis that distills itself into a type of anxiety. This will remain until he is able to resolve the conflict within himself satisfactorily. The co-dependent person will generally not use moral anxiety in the same manner. He is much more likely to envision possible things happening in his life that will probably cause him some more problems and the accompanying anxiety. Again, he is not dealing with matters as they are but as he may see them happening in the future.

Most anxiety is fraught with two major fallacies. First, in many cases we do not really know whether the event will in fact occur. Second, there is no way that we can accurately predict the outcome. Based upon these premises, a great deal of anxiety does not deal with reality, but rather with conjecture and speculation.

Anxiety is tailor-made for co-dependent people. They are accustomed to living and dealing with the world of fantasy and make-believe. Much of their efforts are directed toward avoiding reality. Since anxiety exists largely in that world, they naturally find themselves caught up in it. Second, the co-dependent's feelings, and particularly the shame-bound feelings of being bad, translate themselves into beliefs that bad things will happen. This is the coin in which anxiety trades. The healthy person looks forward optimistically to what is happening in his life, while co-dependents constantly worry about what's going to happen tomorrow. Anxiety in the co-dependent person almost always deals with negative outcomes. He has become so inured to this type of thinking that he cannot envision good things happening.

Anxiety of the unhealthy variety can have some negative effects on the bearer. Many studies have been done in the past decade establishing a link between a person's state of mind and physical condition. This can mean less effective performance on the job. Anxiety will distract the person from the task at hand and keep him from giving his best at that time.

Example. We talked to one young executive, Jim, who suffered from anxiety in his work. Every day Jim felt like something bad was just about to happen. He lived like this for several years, finally accepting it as normal, at least for him. Then one day the anxiety got worse. He became afraid he was not going to escape from his own fears this time. He became afraid of being afraid, i.e., afraid he would not be able to make the "bad" feelings go away. It was like he was going crazy. He ended up in a public rest room in the office building where he was working, curled up on the floor. This was a full-blown panic attack. His fears were that he either was going to die or go crazy. There was a numbness around his cheeks and lips, and he felt it moving into his arms and legs. He kept moving his limbs in order to know that he was still alive. Jim spent two days in bed, unable to eat or sleep, before he was finally able to begin functioning normally. His comment afterwards was, "I'd literally rather die than have to go through something like that again." This is anxiety in its extreme form, but one that is not all that uncommon. We do not have any statistics on the number of business people who have this problem. It is, we know, very common with college students.

DEPRESSION

Depression is the feeling that nothing seems to be working right in one's life. It has been said that depression is anger turned inward. We think that depression occurs when normal emotions become unusually distressing, leaving the person feeling helpless and hopeless. There are gradations of depression, ranging from mild through clinical to suicidal.

If the definition sounds like the inner workings of a shame-bound person, it is because that person usually carries around feelings of depression. How can a person feel good when she feels that she is bad? Feelings of shame are often misdiagnosed as depression, and the symptom is treated rather than the cause.

When we look at depression, we see a person who has quit coping. She may have tried and failed, or she may feel that she is simply not up to it. Her past efforts may have resulted in such dismal outcomes that she does not want to try anymore. Depression is insidious. It can begin in a very small way and grow over a period of time to where the person cannot cope with what is going on in her daily life. While studies show that depression is more common for women, they certainly do not have an exclusive franchise. It affects both sexes and people at nearly any age.

And depression tends to feed upon itself. Once entrenched, it tends to multiply. What may have originally affected only one part of a person's life can become the grim shadow in which her entire existence is spun out.

> **Example.** Marj used to like to go to work. She had a job she really liked and took a lot of pride in it. Then her husband got transferred to another state. Marj had a difficult time making a connection with a new job she could truly enjoy. She had a series of jobs but never felt quite right in any of them. She began to feel inadequate and stupid about herself and wondered if she would ever find anything she liked or could do well enough. She became fearful that, when she grew old, she would not have any pension to support her. All of this worked inside her. She went nearly a year before she told anyone about these negative feelings. She did not want to be a burden on anyone else. Besides, everyone always just said something like "Just get busy. Forget about all that stuff." Finally she read an article in a magazine that described her perfectly. The writer, a woman, had clinical depression. The course of her own feelings paralleled Marj's almost exactly. Once she could understand what was going on in her life, she began to get better by doing some things to take care of herself. Marj, incidentally, was a textbook co-dependent, something she had known and worked on for several years.

CHAPTER 6

HOW SHAME IS MAINTAINED

Are some people just born with shame? Are there some genetic markers predisposing some of us to this? Probably not. At least there is no evidence of this today. If we accept this premise, then something has to happen during our lifetimes that creates the shame we carry with us. It is the same within organizations: something occurs that brings about the shame, and certain things happen that help keep it in place.

We believe shame is just another one of our emotions. It occurs in all of us with some degree of regularity. We experience it when we feel humiliated over something we have done or said, or when somehow our sense of dignity has been offended. It is not like guilt because we have broken no rules. To feel shame is to be human. It is not comfortable, but it is not necessarily debilitating or fatal.

Shame actually can be healthy for us (Bradshaw 1988). It can be the agent of change, the turning point on some issue in our lives. We may grow or become more creative as a result of shame. Healthy shame comes along, is with us for a little while, and then leaves. Sometimes the source corrects itself, and at other times we change in such a way that the feeling is gone.

Recognizing shame can be even more important in an organization. When it has been caught in some shameful situation — whether it be legal, ethical, or just some embarrassing management mistake made public — there is often a change in leadership. This allows the organization the opportunity to face and move past its shame in a way that individuals do not have available to them. The individual is stuck with whoever he is. The organization, however, can use new management to make the needed changes without having to participate in or share

55

the shameful feelings itself. Thus, organizations are much freer to look at the problem and change it.

Like our other emotions, shame can get out of hand. When it does, problems arise. There is, however, a very significant difference: most other emotions affect some particular part of our personality; shame affects the total personality. It is the centerpiece around which other emotions form constellations. It becomes the core of who we are as humans.

If shame can be healthy, what happens to convert it into something unhealthy? We believe that shame left unresolved tends to become pathological. If we are unable or unwilling to deal with feelings of shame within a reasonable time, those feelings become "bad." When we try to deal with some random feeling or event and find that we have little effect on it, we often tend to attach greater importance to it. So we try to make this feeling go away and, when we are unable to do so, assume it must be important or it would not still be there. This is the law of reverse effect: the things that we must get rid of remain, and those we desperately must have elude us. Thus, initially we often overstate the importance of shame in our lives. It becomes more than it really is. And this is a repetitive pattern with shame-bound people in trying to deal with life's events: they blow up things totally out of proportion.

Since we have concluded that shame is indeed important, we will try to examine it more closely to see if it has some hidden meaning or significance for us. Here we are not looking at it to get rid of it; we are interested in the process.

As humans, when we begin to have the feelings associated with shame, we generally focus more of our energy on this feeling, give it more of our attention. The more we examine it, the larger it looks. Since shame consists of feelings of inadequacy about ourselves, we naturally start to look at the other feelings created by the emotion. The feeling is there, the thinking goes, and since it is obviously very important, it must mean that something is essentially wrong with us. If we are particularly unlucky, about this time we will have some other big life events that will fuel this fire. Then these feelings of shame will be neatly lined up with what we already have. And looking at them we will say "By God! I was right. There really is something going on here. Something is really wrong. I need to spend some more time on this."

Once we have become intellectually convinced that something is wrong with our feeling, it has a very good chance to become a part of who we are. When this feeling is in place in our personality, it continues to grow. What would otherwise have been viewed as normal, healthy feelings in the past will henceforth be seen as further evidence of our basic character flaws. A person at this time usually will not consciously call this shame. A lot of the underlying process we have described takes place in the unconscious. He will simply be aware that some things are changing and that he is not as comfortable as before. What happens inside us to block our efforts to rid ourselves of shame? We think four elements contribute to this: reinforcement, repression, association, and distraction.

REINFORCEMENT

First, when a person experiences a shameful event, previous feelings of shame are reinforced. This may happen through an accumulation of similar shameful events that cause the problem to take on an added dimension. In this situation our person is trying to deal with the original problem and continually finds himself swamped by a series of new, but like, events. He does not always see these as related, but tends to view them as separate issues. Reinforcement can also occur through the acts or words of others. For example, a person might perform some act only to have others tell him how bad that it was. Since it is constantly in front of him, he has a hard time getting rid of it.

> *Example.* The most common example we see is with small children. They are constantly bombarded with negative messages about their behavior. "Bad boy." "If you do that mommy will not love you." These constant reinforcements make the child feel he really is bad when he falls short of parental expectation. We think it is reasonable to assume the shame process begins very early with most youngsters. In both her books we have referenced to, Alice Miller has some excellent discussion about how we raise children.

> *Example.* We also see this same type of dynamic at work in businesses. One interesting example came up not too long ago. Todd wanted to get rid of one of his employees, Rusty. Rusty had been around for some time but just was not really doing his work lately. He had always been marginal, and he knew that he was not any great

bargain. But he had always tried to do enough to hold on. Todd was one of those employers who hated confrontation. So what he would do was to try to make Rusty uncomfortable enough that Rusty would decide to leave on his own. He would make oblique, never direct, comments about Rusty's work in sales meetings. He would give Rusty the worst assignments. Rusty was not particularly good, but he was tenacious, and he held on. As time passed, this whole dance continued. The result was that Rusty finally had to leave. And he was very hurt and angry with what had happened. The constant sniping at him had taken a toll on his self-esteem. It had not made Todd feel very good either. The shame Rusty had before was maintained and intensified during this period.

REPRESSION

The second thing that may happen is that the act may be repressed. By this we mean that the feeling is simply pushed out of the consciousness into the person's unconscious. Some things in life are just so painful that we cannot deal with them in the here and now. So the mind puts them aside by stuffing the feelings inside, taking them away from our awareness so we will not have to confront them. This is not necessarily bad in every situation, as we will see later when we discuss defense mechanisms more thoroughly. But when this becomes a way of life, then a pathological condition sets in.

When this happens, the shameful deed is beyond reach and cannot be expiated through some constructive act we might take. It becomes a secret, sometimes even a secret from ourselves. Secrets have a tendency to grow out of proportion to reality. Over time they take on an almost mystical quality. If we step back and look at our past histories, most of us will see that the secrets we have chosen to share with others seem, in retrospect, fairly harmless. Dealing with an issue in the present moment deflates its importance; hanging on to it exaggerates its real meaning. And the longer we hold on, the bigger the problem seems and the harder it is to release.

We see this very commonly with sexual events one has experienced as a child. They are so fraught with "badness" that the person simply cannot deal with them. More and more today we see women who have been the victims of sexual abuse during their early years and simply have no present memory of it. The event, however, continues to have a very profound influence on their lives and how they relate to others, especially in areas involving their own romantic lives or in attitudes conveyed to their children.

> *Example.* This can also happen with businesses and individuals within those businesses. One we saw some time ago was an executive who had been fired from his last job. He had had a responsible position but simply had been turned loose by the board of directors. He wandered around for some time and then finally found another position in another industry. He began like a lamb but before long was prowling like a lion. He had totally forgotten his past bad experiences. In chemical dependency counseling we call this "euphoric recall," remembering only the good parts, and that was the same thing that was happening here. This particular person talked a lot about his past successes without ever mentioning any of the more unfortunate things that had happened. It was as though his life had been one long glide along the road of success. He was never able to confront his darker side, those issues that had caused him a lot of shame at one time. Rather, he was still caught in his shame-bound feelings but was out of touch with the causes.

ASSOCIATION

The third thing we see happening is the process by which some events take on added meaning through connections, or associations, with previous things that have happened to us.

> *Example.* The last time Sara made a mistake at work, her boss chewed her out in public. Now even the possibility of another mistake dredges up all those feelings of shame and embarrassment. This association causes her a great deal of anxiety with an event that is really pretty harmless. But when she experiences something in the present that recalls an uncomfortable time from the past, those same feelings occur. What may have begun as healthy shame is transformed into destructive shame.

Rather than working through the shame, the person usually chooses to ignore it. She has the common human tendency to believe if she ignores something that causes pain or creates problems, that it will magically go away. And for this person the shame does in fact seem to disappear. The problem is that she has simply transferred it from her consciousness to her unconscious, where it will join the other accumulated shame.

DISTRACTION

The final way we neglect dealing with shame is through distraction. *Distraction* occurs when we focus our attention in some other direction rather than addressing the real problem. Rather than dealing with healthy shame issues, we ignore them.

This can happen at different levels. We want to become distracted, so we actively seek a method or vehicle to accomplish this. This is very similar to an interaction between two people where one really works hard to change the subject from something that is uncomfortable. The only difference here is that the process only involves one person and takes place within that person's mind.

This also happens when a real-life event of greater significance comes along and we have a strong need to pursue it. If a person were, for example, humiliated over some trivial thing, and, while trying to get it worked out, a close family member became seriously ill or died, the humiliated person would naturally shift her focus to the new problem. Since the first event was relatively unimportant by comparison, she is quite unlikely to return to it. The problem is that her feelings about it remain, thus allowing it to filter through her mental system and become a part of her bag of tricks.

> *Example.* Co-dependents are great at creating distractions. It is often said that if there is not a crisis, a co-dependent will create one. Within an organization this can happen in any number of ways. The most common means we have seen used is for the person to become a workaholic.
>
> Beth worked in a retail store as a salesclerk. She had had a lot of problems at home with her alcoholic husband and a teenage son who was constantly in trouble. It seemed that no matter what she did, nothing changed. Work became a distraction for her. During the few hours each day when she was at work, she did not have to deal with either of the men in her life. She did her job very well and received a lot of praise. This satisfied some of her needs for acceptance, which she did not get at home. As time went by, Beth started working longer hours, even coming into the store during her time off. She had found a refuge from the problems at home and in so doing had substituted work for her co-dependency. This was no lasting solution, only a temporary adjustment to a deeper problem. She had become more

and more distracted from the real problem, which was not her husband, her son, or her work. It was herself.

We believe other issues affect and contribute to the shame within us. Some may argue that these could be included under the general headings we have used here. We believe, however, they are important enough to discuss separately. These issues include powerlessness, the past, grief, the future, and fantasies.

POWERLESSNESS

Chief among these issues is the feeling of powerlessness. We are using this word advisedly, for we discuss control and power elsewhere. What we mean here is that the person feels he has no influence on the direction his life is taking. He will often describe this as being "out of control."

As he looks around him, this person will see other people who appear to have their lives together. When he compares what he feels and sees happening in his life with those of others, he feels hopeless and helpless. Of course, the fallacy in this thinking is that he is only seeing the outside appearance of others, many who are wearing masks in public to hide the panic within. The saying in treatment centers is that "I wanted to be on the inside like you looked on the outside." Once this feeling of powerlessness has taken hold, it can invade other areas of life. It can create anxiety that in turn creates more anxiety — afraid of being afraid — which can result in disabling a person through panic. Or it may bring on depression, the final step of which can be suicide.

As one feels his life slipping away, as he feels he is losing "control" in his life today, he quite often moves out of the here and now into the past or future or fantasy world. Since one has only a certain amount of energy available, to the extent that he expends it with old business, future events, or fantasies, he robs today. Today's realities are neglected.

Example. Many people have moments when they feel powerless, when events in life or someone around them is out of control. Tim worked in a business that was examined by government regulators. Government regulation was just part of the industry. Tim had never really cared for these people, but had tolerated them because they were a fact of life. The regulatory people knew of his attitude. Once when he made a big issue of one of their decisions and won by appealing to the district office, one of the field men told him, "You won this time. But we will get you SOBs next time." Tim did not worry too much about this. Then the day came when something went wrong in the business. The regulators leapt on this and used it as a means to force Tim's resignation. Tim was not culpable of anything except bad judgment. However, the regulators gave interviews to the newspapers, implying he had done something wrong, perhaps criminal. Nothing ever came of these accusations since they had no factual basis, but Tim was heavily shamed, and that took a long time to heal. And he felt totally helpless to fight back. Engaging a regulatory agency in battle is somewhat like trying to put a cloud into a bottle — there is nothing to get hold of.

THE PAST

A very significant number of people, on a daily basis, live most of their lives in the past. They are caught up in what has gone before. Much of what they think about each day has to do with "if onlys": "If only I had done this or that or thought of something different to do at the time." They have a tendency to go back and replay old scenes over and over to try to see how they might have had some different outcome. They will actually redialogue conversations and imagine different outcomes. While they do this, they totally ignore the present. Much of what they ruminate upon in the past has to do with what they see as slights or harms or injustices done to them by others, or caused by some events, or how they might have done something differently that would have created different outcomes. The problem is that these are only memories, and no amount of replaying will allow them to change what has already happened.

To the extent that they engage in this type of behavior, they rob today of its full value. And then today becomes another yesterday, filled with disappointments because they have not gotten what they think their full measure should be. These disappointments tend to pile up day after day, and so this type of problem is neither one shot nor static; rather, it tends to be cumulative and becomes worse with time. Its nature is progressive. It acts like a whirlpool, carrying them deeper and deeper into its destructive pattern of behavior. After a while they find themselves spending a lot more time in the past than in the present.

The result is that they lose touch with what is going on around them today and live silently in yesteryear.

Generally, we have found that always looking over one's shoulder means that the person is angry and resentful about the hand she has been dealt in life. She dwells on the negative features of her existence. Anger itself can actually be a healthy feeling. It can be a motivator for our lives. However, the type of anger we get from ruminating in the past is not healthy. It deals with events that are only historical, ones that can never be changed.

When anger is taken and carefully nourished, it becomes resentment or, occasionally, rage. Moreover, a resentment does not give us any energy to move forward but keeps us a captive of the past. Resentment operates at a very subtle level, often outside the consciousness of the person. But it tends to be very pervasive and affects other important areas of life.

We are not saying the past is unimportant. Certainly it has shaped and molded who we are today. We just think that being stuck in yesteryear is a terrible waste of human resources. Yalom put this into perspective when he said that the past is important in the present against the landscape of the future (1975, p. 176).

So we want to add anger and resulting resentment to the list of the causes of shame. When the co-dependent views these fixtures of the past, they become monuments to failure. Our person sees how she has failed in some past undertaking and tries to correct it by reliving it now. Of course, she will never get what she is seeking. In fact, her very efforts will only add further to her sense of frustration and failure. The sought-after cure becomes a part of the problem.

We can learn from the past, but we cannot change it. Trying to do so results in a continuing sense of frustration.

> **Example.** The past takes an enormous toll from the present. Millie had a series of jobs over the past several years. For some people this would probably be fun since it always allowed for something new in life. Actually she lived in a small resort town where people typically worked more than one job, and there was a lot of movement from one job to another. What was happening to her was fairly typical of what happened to most people in this community. But for Millie it had come to represent failure. She felt now as though she would

never be able to get and keep a job she liked. When we saw her, she had reached a point where she was almost paralyzed with fear. She was afraid that the next job she worked at would turn out like all the rest and she would be on the street looking again. This had become so much of a problem that she was even afraid to apply for work. She spent a lot of time looking at the want ads and circling those ads that looked interesting to her. But she could not get up the courage to call and make an appointment for an interview.

Millie was truly a captive of the past. Her experiences in her work had pushed her into a personal system of shame-bound feelings, a place where she had lost her own sense of self-worth and identity as a worthwhile employee. In turn, this affected not only her performance on the job, but even her courage to apply for one.

GRIEF

Along with other feelings a person has about the past, there is often a sense of loss over what might have been. The realization that whatever is in the past cannot be recaptured and that those opportunities are lost forever often sets up a grief process. Sometimes a loss of innocence supports feelings of sadness.

We do not propose to explore this phenomenon in any depth. The stages of grief have been described by Kubler-Ross as denial, anger, bargaining, depression, and acceptance (1969). If one experiences a sense of loss and does not allow the process to work its way through, she will end up with unresolved grief. This can be part of what keeps a person stuck in the past. If she is able to resolve this grief and finally let go of her past, she can get on with the business of the present.

In dealing with people who are chemically dependent we often see this inability to grieve the loss of the substance they are giving up. These people often get stuck in either the anger or depression phase and are never really able to move into an acceptance stage. This sometimes sets the person up for relapse. Likewise, when a person has shame-bound feelings and is unable to resolve the grief surrounding them, she is likely to have more problems in the future. Grief occurs when she realized that she is not presently, nor will she ever be, "normal" in the sense that others are. Letting go of this is a process that takes time and occurs in describable stages.

Example. Judy's husband had been very successful in his business. Then came the day when he had a number of financial reverses. They all happened at one time, and as a result he lost all of his money and had to declare bankruptcy. For Judy this was a terrible day. She had gotten very used to living a life-style that only money could provide. Besides, it was a major embarrassment to have her husband's name in the paper where all his financial woes were on display to the world. A couple of years after all of this happened Judy's husband was in a new job and happily employed, although he was now making considerably less money than before. About that time Judy began to have some depression and was having a hard time being around her old friends. In counseling it came out that she had never let go of her old life-style. She had been unable to grieve the loss of what had happened, to let go of what had been before, and to move through it to a stage of accepting her new life as it actually was. As a result she still was carrying some of her old grief along with a good measure of shame from the past, all of which came out in her as depression.

THE FUTURE

Also laden with problems is the future. We tend to fear what we do not know or understand, and our crystal ball is never clear enough to accurately predict the future. So it is necessarily fraught with unknowns. Because of this it can become the source of great fear.

If the past is the realm of "if only," then the future can be characterized as the world of "what if?". Co-dependents are adept at playing this mind game with themselves. They project themselves into the future and begin to script events somewhere "out there." They actually go through imaginary conversations with other people, weighing what they will say, speculating on what others will say in return, and then forming their responses to that. Then they begin to look at alternatives to the conversation and map them out also. This is a never-ending process. Of course, it very, very rarely goes as they had planned. And then that encounter moves behind them, slides into the past, and enters the realm of "if only." From this they make a decision that they will not allow this to happen to them again, that next time they will plan even better. And so they do just that. They script their next encounter even more carefully, trying to use the knowledge of the last event to improve their outlook this time. And the results are assuredly the same.

These two feed upon and into one another, setting up a self-perpetuating cycle. The problem, of course, is that either is destructive, but together they are an almost unbeatable combination. People who are co-dependent have become masters at staying caught up in these two time frames. Both rob energy from today, and both deal with the world in an unreal way. The past is but memories, and the future is only dreams. The only reality is here and now, what is happening to each of us in this moment. To the extent that we rob this present time of our energy, we do not give it the best we have to offer. It is really sad to see people going through life with so little investment in the present, always bitter about the past and fearful of the future.

> **Example.** We knew one person, Scott, who spent his life making lists about what he was going to do in the future. In fact, he was so occupied with this chore each day that he did not have time to do anything else. His whole existence was tied to the future. He had been out of work for several months when we first encountered him. His wife was working hard to keep the family together. When anyone mentioned to Scott that it seemed what he was doing was largely an exercise, he became very defensive and angry. Scott had traded in his present existence for a slice of what he hoped the future might hold. But the chances of failure were so real to him and frightening that he was never able to execute any of his plans. In his case just thinking about failing created shame for him.

The fascinating part about people such as Scott is that they have no idea what is truly going on. Their focus has become so future-oriented that they are unable to see what is happening around them today. This allows them to shut off the shame breeding out of their total lack of any meaning in their lives today. They truly believe, as Scarlett O'Hara did, that everything will be okay tomorrow.

FANTASIES

We had thought for a long time that most of our timing problems were associated with the past and future. Recently a client suggested that he had another problem: the world of fantasy. That seemed to make a lot of sense when we looked at it in the context of the other two areas. Both the past and the future represent places that are not presently real, and the fantasy world is just more of the same. And so why not include fantasies in with them?

The important point to be made here is that whenever we engage in behavior that distracts us from the present, we run the risk of using our available energy for some useless purpose. Then how are we going to deal with the world of fantasy? We all have fantasies. They are important in our lives since they allow us to live out certain feelings without actually having to engage in the behavior. Thus, they act more or less as a safety valve for expression of feelings and help us guard against behavior that otherwise might be unacceptable. For example, if you are really angry with some other person, you might have a fantasy about beating him up. Having this fantasy does no one harm. But if each of us had to act out each one of these feelings, the result would be chaos.

So as we looked at this issue, the key question was how were we to deal with fantasies since they are such a real part of life? It seemed logical that the goal was to strike some balance between healthy fantasies and those that become destructive. There might be several ways to determine how this line is to be drawn. We suggest that whenever fantasies begin to get in the way of a person's living his life fully and being able to accomplish the things he truly needs and wants to do, then it has become a problem. If the fantasies take over and dictate behavior, or if one has a hard time separating fantasies from reality, it is time for a change. This sounds suspiciously like a good definition of addictive behavior. And when you think of how fantasies cause problems, perhaps this does make some sense.

> **Example.** We talked recently to Richard, a managerial type who worked for a very peculiar man named Ed. Ed had worked his way into a family-owned business that had done exceptionally well. He had become president of the company. Ed's behavior at best could be described as bizarre, but in this company it sounded more like diagnosable paranoia. Ed did not trust his employees. He had surrounded himself with a small band of loyal executives in whom he confided, but beyond this group he had little communication with employees. He would occasionally call an employee in, throw some paper at him or her, and demand to know what this meant. He also felt employees should not be paid very much, notwithstanding the fact the company was performing very well and Ed's salary was

$300,000. Ed was a tyrant in the office and was thoroughly hated by employees. He also had some ethical issues with insider dealing between his parent company and some service companies in which he had a personal financial stake. Richard told us that one of the favorite pastimes of employees in this company was to share their fantasies about Ed. There were some rather innovative ways people had devised to deal with him. It seemed to us that a lot of corporate time went into this game, time that could have been used productively in making money for the company. Ed had fostered a situation where employees in part ducked the realities of day-to-day work to enjoy the escape these fantasies provided them.

Fantasies generally do not take over. One interesting thing we have noticed about fantasies is that they tend to be repetitious, at least insofar as the subject matter is concerned. There may be some variations on how it is mentally acted out, but the issue generally remains constant. This was the case with Ed and his employees. He was the center of attention; the only thing that changed was the way in which the fantasizer was going to get even with him.

CHAPTER 7

COPING MECHANISMS

In order to understand the specific coping mechanisms we will be discussing, we need first to cover a couple particulars. We need to look at the nature of defense mechanisms generally, and, since from this point forward we will be looking at the individual and corporate psyche in some similar, interchangeable ways, we need to lay some groundwork showing the similarities between them.

A *defense mechanism* is a technique used by a person to deal with material in his life that is presently unacceptable. Defense mechanisms generally help humanity retain its collective sanity. We are constantly bombarded with information, some of which is unacceptable to us. If we had to take all of that in and process it consciously, we would either be totally consumed with this activity or, more likely, our minds would short circuit. We have a real investment in maintaining some order in our lives, some balance, and, properly applied, defense mechanisms allow us to accomplish this.

There are times, however, when one or more of these defense mechanisms, for one reason or another, become too powerful. The result is that we are effectively blocked off from reality. What had been a weapon, our friend, has now become an enemy. Defense mechanisms are very rarely, if in fact ever, available to us at a conscious level. They exist somewhere below the level of consciousness, floating in the vast realm of the unconscious. As such, we are not aware of when they are at work. By the same token, we are unaware of when they have shifted their roles from one of protection to one of harm. So even if we were to want to guard against the illegitimate roles defense mechanisms are capable of assuming, we are largely without tools to identify and accomplish this.

When we talk about the psyche, we are describing both the conscious and unconscious parts of the personality of a person or an organization. It comprises all those parts that come together to form someone or something we can describe as unique. We suggest that both people and organizations have a psyche. Since organizations arise as the expressions of people, in the beginning they are imprinted with the personalities of those who make up and operate them. In the case of especially small organizations, this may continue to be true. We believe, however, that over time, as an organization grows larger and as there are a succession of different people parading through it, the organization itself begins to take on a personality. To be sure, some particularly strong individuals or dramatic events may leave their imprint on the organization from time to time, but the entity proceeds forward through time largely on its own inertia.

While there are some differences between the development of the psyche in the individual and in an organization, they are not particularly relevant at this point. We arrive in this world, largely without a personality (except to the extent we accept a theory like Jung's thoughts about a collective unconscious). We are bombarded with the ideas and beliefs of others, mainly family. Shortly, we begin to form our own unique personality and use it to guide us through life. It may be altered by some exceptional person or event, but it is something that is essentially our own and that to a large degree is unaffected by outside forces.

The whole idea of similarities between individual and organizational psyches is consistent with the general systems approach to life discussed later. The experience of any living system, whether a person or some group, is linked to those of other living systems and has some commonality with others wherever they may occur in the hierarchy.

DENIAL

The one essential ingredient supporting any addiction is denial. *Denial* may be defined as a refusal or present inability to accept observable facts as reality. This is the belief that "nothing's wrong with me." It is a defense mechanism that is very powerful and very clever.

Denial is one of the most potent defenses available to the human psyche. It can literally turn day into night. The ability to refuse to acknowledge what is so readily apparent to others allows our minds to effectively block out any material that is not otherwise dealt with through assimilation or by use of other, less potent defenses.

The other characteristic of denial is its progressive nature. Through studies of addictive behavior, we have learned that as the disease progresses in its intensity, denial by the victim also progresses, apparently paralleling the course of the addiction. So there is always a sufficient amount of denial available to subvert the truth, no matter how severe the symptoms become.

We believe that this progressive nature of denial is also present when dealing with co-dependent and shame-bound behavior. As the amount and intensity of shame increase through usage and time, denial maintains the pace. The affected person does not have the slightest notion about what is going wrong, no matter how bad things become. Addictive behavior is simply one symptom of the shame-bound problem. There is neither evidence nor reason to believe that denial works any differently than do other behavioral manifestations of shame, and empirical clinical data tends to bear this out.

Within an organization, denial takes on several different forms. Perhaps one catchall for this is the idea of company loyalty. It is widely believed that if you work for an organization, you owe it unquestioning allegiance. To criticize is to step over clearly drawn boundary lines.

Example. Phillip was the owner of his own service company. He had started literally without anything and with a great deal of work had built his company up into something that earned him a good living. He was apparently happy with this for some time but then began to look around and see some of his friends who were living in larger homes and driving more expensive cars. Phillip had relied upon two people to direct a lot of business his way and approached them to see if they would allow him to join in some of their ventures as an investor. They did this, and after a time Phillip began his own business ventures. In the process of becoming wealthy Phillip had to borrow a lot of money. He thought this was okay since he was always able to repay it on time. During the economic downswing of the 1980s Phillip could no longer service his loans. He was forced to sell a lot of his assets. He even had to let go of his dream 12,000-square-foot home.

He started losing everything. The point of the story is not the bad luck Phillip had. When all of this happened, he turned on those who had helped and supported him through the years. He claimed they had forced him into their investments, even made him a partner in some of them. Further, they had arranged for him to borrow money he did not want to finance these operations. As time went on and the truth became more apparent to all, Phillip was more insistent in his denial. Insofar as we know, Phillip still, in his own mind, believes all of this nonsense. He is one of the best examples we have seen of complete, total denial. He simply could not face the idea that he may have made some mistakes, some errors of judgment. They simply had to be someone else's fault.

And so we see dynamics develop that do not differ materially from those describing dysfunctional families. Loyalty is translated into a conspiracy of silence that members are expected to obey. Superficial problems may be approached with caution; problems that reach the heart and soul of an organization simply remain buried under layers of denial. Even if a person were to attempt to ferret out the sources of discontent, the defensive coating is so multilayered and well protected that he would only succeed in removing one transparent strip, much like successively removing layers of an onion.

Coupled with silence are a multitude of rules, regulations, and policies. Such rules, regulations, and policies usually begin with some legitimate purpose. As time goes on, organizations use this vehicle for many single-purpose objectives totally unrelated to overall organizational policy and direction. Thus, we find that organizations can effectively block or detour any genuine efforts to probe deeply into their corporate psyche. This is really no different from what the mind does for the individual through denial. It allows the corporation to avoid confronting its own reality through the institutionalization of such procedures.

Example. Perhaps the best example one can find is within the government sector. As we begin to gain more access to information through the Freedom of Information Act, we see just how much our government has sought in the past to cover up its own mistakes and embarrassments through the use of classification of documents and records. Many of the issues we now see cause us a feeling of national shame. Before, we allowed our officials to hide these things from us largely in the interest of "national defense." Indeed, the Nixon administration sought to use this device to cover up its own misdeeds and irregularities.

If shame in individuals takes on its own life form, then it really thrives in an organizational structure. First, organizations have a life of their own separate from those who are a part of it. Unlike the individual, an organization has virtually no terminal point. It continues on and on. Second, its component parts in the form of human beings are constantly changing. This is a far cry from a single human being who, while certainly changing over time, does not experience alterations in psyche in the same manner as the modern business corporation does in its collective personality.

We have said that denial in the human lies below the level of awareness, somewhere in the unconscious. And so it is with a business. In the case of the latter, denial is even harder to treat since there is a constant metamorphosis of the corporate personality. Even attempting to isolate and define the corporate person at any given point in time is certain to be frustrating.

Companies are also very good at compartmentalization. Unlike some systems where there is always synergistic interplay among the various components, companies can take areas and totally isolate them from other functioning parts. Sometimes it becomes convenient to isolate shame-based beliefs and behaviors in an area where, while they continue to affect overall company health, they are largely out of sight and beyond the reach of most other units within the organization. Is this then a conscious effort? We do not know. It may have been so in the first place, perhaps an attempt to bury some company secret that was the source of embarrassment or shame. But through attrition and change in personnel, the company may not consciously be aware of what happened in the past. The reasons for cubbyholing by past generations may be lost on today's employees. Nonetheless, shame is effectively buried within the company and is a disease that continues to spread its virus throughout the organization.

PERFECTIONISM

Along with denial is the issue of perfectionism. This is an attempt by some shame-bound person to prove that he's okay by always doing everything right. Because he sees his life as largely out of control, he believes that if he is only able to perform in a superior fashion every time, it will make him feel worthwhile.

The first problem, of course, is that our person is looking for his own self-worth in the wrong place. Since shame is an internal matter that affects the person at the heart of his personhood, it is impossible to get the much-needed remedial help from outside sources. Shame moves from the inside out, not vice versa. Outside events may actually foster the problem of shame by helping the person feel good for a period of time, but they cannot remedy the basic feeling of being no good. Of course, the person who is shame-bound is not able to see or understand this. His feelings of shame are kept well hidden from himself by his own denial. Some event that occurs externally cannot offset the energized internal feelings the person has. But he will keep reaching for something, somewhere to fix himself.

> *Example.* Fran believed when he came to work that everything had to been done just right. This was not something he acquired when he arrived on the job. He had had this feeling most of his life. He simply carried this baggage to work with him. Oftentimes things did not work out as he had planned. For him, doing the job right meant doing it in such a way that it turned out as he had planned. And was he surprised. When he began working within an organization and with other people, things often turned out very differently. Fran was extremely frustrated with this. He saw the inability to make it work his way as a personal failure.

The real problem with perfectionism is that it will never work. To be human is, by definition, to be imperfect. There may be times when we match or even exceed our own expectations. When this happens, we get a great high. But there are also times when we will fall short of the mark. This is inevitable.

In the shame-bound person, because he either fails or refuses to acknowledge this reality, he continues to strive for perfection. This striving is itself a setup for failure. If he continues to set unrealistic goals and continues to reach for them with the expectation that he might achieve them, he must necessarily fail at times. Again, the shame-bound person is so caught up in a web of denial that he doesn't see this.

Consider what happens. I feel bad somehow. I believe that if I can succeed in whatever I am doing I will feel better. The more successful I am, the better chance I have of feeling okay. If only I can do this task perfectly, I will be completely okay. I undertake the project and fall short of my goal. I have failed. I feel embarrassed and ashamed of my own performance. Thus, the very means by which I figured to solve my problem has become yet another brick in my wall of shame.

We have noted before that shame-bound people typically take small events and magnify their importance beyond any reasonable proportions. In this case our person will translate failing at a task as being a failure, and will take that into his internal self as a perceived statement of fact. It is interesting to watch this person. Again, it is as though he has a set of binoculars. The least important things get magnified, and with events that are truly important he reverses the lenses so that they become nonevents.

When this process of feeling failure occurs, the only logical way for our person to solve this is by performing perfectly in the future, or perhaps choosing more complicated chores to perform. At times, simply performing at the same level of competency may become redundant, a mere scorekeeping exercise. Somehow the belief is that as the individual is able to perform perfectly on more intense or complex tasks, it will help erase the failures of the past and act as a type of counterbalance. Of course, what happens is that he continues to perform at different levels of competency at different times. So instead of solving his problem, he merely adds to it. As the tasks increase in severity, the chances of failure are enhanced. As time goes on, he becomes more driven, more compulsive about succeeding.

This compulsion can become obsessive over time and may present itself as a true pathological problem. While there are all types and degrees of this behavior, in business the most common is the workaholic. The workaholic is by definition a person addicted to work. He sees his work as a way of validating himself, again that reaching outside himself to cure his feelings of inadequacy.

Example. Stories about workaholics are legion, and while the whole issue has been written about extensively, we choose to give a single example of this type of person. Max ran his own business. He had spent a number of years learning his trade, and now, finally, he had a chance to succeed on his own. He really threw himself into his work. He spent long hours at the shop and drove himself unmercifully. No matter how much he worked, he always felt as though he had more to do. Over time, Max began to link his personal worth with how well the business did. If he had a good month, he was fine. If it had been bad, he was depressed. His whole life revolved around the job. And finally his whole personality became so intertwined with his business that no one could separate the two. Max had become a workaholic. This was something more than simply working a lot. It was where he drew personal value from his work. Everyone does this to some extent. With Max, it had become a sickness.

The whirlpool into which our shame-bound person has fallen draws him deeper and deeper into his own shame and what he sees as shame-producing behavior. This is circular and mutually reinforcing. Without some type of intervention it will continue until he dies.

Business organizations feed into this process almost perfectly. They continually impose unrealistic goals and expectations on people. As if the individual did not have his own problems of perfectionism, he now has another important player in his life telling him that he needs to be perfect. Corporate strategies push for maximum performance — and beyond.

Example. We think the best example that can be given about perfectionism comes from the area of company performance and profitability. While every business has difficulties in its organizational life, there is often a management mind-set that if the company's performance this year is superior, all other problems will pale into insignificance and magically go away. So management often puts unrealistic goals on employees to perform constantly at higher and higher levels. This is not unlike the parent who demands and expects his or her children to continue to excel. This presents a double bind to the employees. If they fall short of the goal, they have failed; if they succeed, they are pushed to even higher and often unrealistic limits the next time. It is a place where they can never truly succeed in the truest sense of the word. Performance has become not a goal, but a sentence for failure.

Business falls into the same trap as do individuals. When it falls short, its collective psyche cannot allow it to accept responsibility, so it pushes the problem to lower echelons within the organization. We will explore the issue of blame in the next section.

Organizations are notorious for their methods of dealing with failures. At one end of the spectrum is firing, and at the other end totally ignoring the person and/or the problem. There are all sorts of imaginable gradations in between. The point is this: organizations see falling short of the mark as failure and cannot deal with it any more effectively than individuals can. They must transfer their collective feelings somewhere else. That somewhere generally becomes individual employees.

Individuals within organizations live with an almost constant fear and anxiety about failure. When they do not measure up to some company expectation, they feel a sense of personal failure. This is soon reinforced through organizational scorn heaped upon them for letting the company down. This whole load is then internalized by the individual and neatly tucked away with other feelings of shame.

BLAME

The third element in this three-sided arrangement is blame. *Blame* is simply where we assess someone else with the responsibility for some action and its consequences, thus avoiding having to accept responsibility. If we are simply assessing this responsibility on a pragmatic, realistic basis, then we should be using the word "accountability." Blame goes beyond rightful allocation of responsibility. It happens when responsibility is shifted from its rightful owner to some other, usually innocent party.

Why does this have to happen? Building upon what we have already seen, we can say that a shame-bound person has a need to be perfect. When something goes wrong in his life, it may mean that whatever it is, he is not perfect. When this happens, our person has to deny any culpability or he feels failure. The easiest way to deal with this is to let someone else assume the responsibility. He does this by blaming someone else. By doing this he is free to move on.

Example. We saw a situation about ten years ago, a time when economic conditions in some parts of the country became severe, where many people turned on others in ways that would have been unimaginable a year or two earlier. People who were partners and co-workers began to blame one another for the losses the organization was incurring when really general financial problems in the community at large were the basic problem. Some of these people became nearly pathological in their anger toward others. In turn, this caused major disruptions in the lives of some of those who, though generally faultless, received most of the blame. Within businesses people scurried about to lay the blame at the doorstep of someone, anyone, else. It was a time of general moral and ethical deterioration. The spiritual reasoning of the players was lost in a sea of self-pity and blaming. The most interesting part of this whole scenario is that only a few weeks before, these same people were great friends and business associates, extending and receiving all types of trust among one another. And then when the going became tough, they turned on one another, each fighting for financial survival.

We were frankly shocked by some of the outcomes of this period. It was probably not really very different from other economic hard times. But we had a grandstand seat and were able to see from close range some of the interactions among the players. And what we saw were some of the very cruel behaviors one person in business can display toward another. There was enormous damage done to some people, especially those who were not strong enough inside to weather the storm of criticism. The irony about this was that many who were most adamant in their self-righteous, self-serving anger were never really able to see the vast damage they had caused in the lives of others.

Corporate hierarchy leads the way in this process. Blaming almost always flows either laterally or, most commonly, downward. Because of the hierarchy, some people at lower levels do not see themselves as able to mount a defense for their actions when blame is directed at them. They are fearful that their bosses will find other ways to deal with them if they object or complain.

In selecting someone to blame, the blamer will rarely pick a strong person. The strong person is more likely to complain. So the person chosen is usually one who is seen as weak. The very characteristics that make a person seem weak may be induced through his own sense of internal shame. Since the scapegoat is generally already caught up in the addiction of shame, he just takes this additional dose and adds it to what he has already stored up. This, of course, is unfair to that person, but, because of his own internal feelings, he is unable to reject the blame directed at him.

> *Example.* One of the most interesting situations we see today is when a company is in legal trouble. Management quickly looks around for a scapegoat. In the recent Drexel Burnham scandal, management seemed content to allow Michael Millken to take the heat for corporate policies. The movie *Wall Street* points up the hypocrisy in corporate life. So long as the young broker was producing, he got all the recognition, including a corner, private office. But when he stubbed his toe and was arrested, the manager (Hal Holbrook) hurried to put distance between himself and the offender, stating that the young man had been too ambitious and that he (the manager) had known this day of reckoning was coming.

The issues of denial, perfectionism, and blame interact. They play off one another and make sense structurally when they are viewed together. These three represent attitudes and behaviors that help support the issue of control. A sense of control, as we will discuss in the next chapter, is seen as so important to the shame-bound person that he develops tools that help shore up this feeling of control. The whole fabric is a sham. The tools do not perform their desired functions; often they produce opposite results. We believe that control itself does not exist in the real sense of the word.

Again, each person has a finite amount of energy. Likewise, the organization, as a system, has a certain amount of energy available to it. When that energy is used to chase fantasies, both the individual and the organization are left with less energy available to accomplish their respective tasks.

Because the struggle for control and the accompanying techniques are viewed as progressive in nature, as time passes, more time and energy will be directed toward chasing this rainbow. The company suffers doubly: it loses worker efficiency and also uses its own collective energy pursuing the same types of illusory goals.

It is hard to quantify the effect this has on a business. We assume that there is a direct economic impact due to loss of productivity. Many of the consequential behaviors flowing out of this exercise will also have adverse effects on the company. Many of these occur at an individual, personal level and are hard to equate in dollars. But the company suffers from employee anger, depression, stress, greed, dependency, cynicism, and arrogance, as well as such things as absenteeism, lack of loyalty, slowdown, and sabotage. These feelings and behaviors not only have an effect on each person who is directly involved, but also on others who have to interact with them. This ripple effect can frustrate productivity and progress.

CHAPTER 8

CONTROL, POWER, SELF-DISCIPLINE, AND INFLUENCE

We believe that as a coping mechanism, control is important enough to merit a chapter of its own. There are some special characteristics about the concept of control that tend to cause a lot of mischief in organizations. Further, it is important to see how the illusion of control is positioned against the realities of power, self-discipline, and influence.

An organization consists of a series of relationships within a living structure that has it own rules and norms and that usually has some objective it tries to accomplish. Control, power, self-discipline, and influence arise within the relationships and, in fact, cannot exist outside of them. So we find these behaviors, to one degree or another, in every organization. These four concepts are somewhat related in their outward manifestations and, thus, are often confused and mistaken for one another. While they do in fact have some commonalities, they differ greatly in terms of reality, legitimacy, and outcomes.

These issues are very important in co-dependency. An understanding of them is essential to seeing the choices people have in personal interactions and how co-dependents, and perhaps others, often spend a lot of their time and energy chasing after something that may not in fact exist.

CONTROL

One of the central issues of co-dependency is control. *Control* is defined as the attempt by one person through force of his own will to manipulate another person or his own environment. The idea is that if a person simply puts his mind and energy to something, he can change it. This is most commonly seen in interactions between people. However, it can occur when the co-dependent uses this same technique in an attempt to control groups, organizations, events, or other parts of the world around him.

Control has great psychological significance to the co-dependent. He sees his life largely in terms of the unfilled cup, often empty and meaningless. He is unable to gain the personal satisfaction or outward recognition he needs through his own accomplishments. He learns that society gives strokes not only for personal accomplishments, but also for how much one person influences or changes others or events.

The problem then becomes how to exert such control that things happen in a way that other people will notice. And so he tries to make things happen in his world. But when he tries to do so, he fails. He simply does not have any base from which to exert his influence nor does he really understand what this means. And so he resorts to magical thinking, to a fantasy that allows him to believe — truly believe — that he is making things happen in his world. This is control. The problem is that it does not actually exist. Thus we see that his efforts to control are not really grounded in reality, rather that they are illusory.

This comes as a shock to most people. In counseling or in group presentations when we talk about the "illusion of control" people initially refuse to accept the phrase and the idea. They say, "I control a lot of things every day. What about controlling myself?" That is all make-believe — magical thinking. To think that we can actually change anything through exerting our will on others or objects, or ourselves for that matter, simply overstates our abilities and potential. To be human implies that we have limitations, and, at least to date insofar as we know, one of these limitations is how much we really can influence the world around us through sheer force of will.

The problem, of course, is that in the mind of the would-be controller, this fantasy is seen as reality. He has such a sense of failure and emptiness in other areas of his life that he retreats to control as a last refuge to salvage his personhood. He wants it to work so badly that he believes it actually does.

The second part of the problem is the legitimacy of control. If we accept the fact that control could only exist in terms of a relationship, then both parties have to be aware of the issue to give it life and substance. Control is a silent process. The controller picks this method precisely because it is an internally generated, unilateral action. All of the choices are exercised by the controller. Force of will is something he does not have to explain or share with anyone, nor is he accountable for the outcome. If he tried to explain what was happening, others would shake their heads or laugh at him. He cannot really explain what is happening when he tries to exert his will for the simple reason that it does not exist. It is an illusion he has created for himself, and, like all illusions, it cannot be isolated and examined in a way that makes sense to others.

We see isolated cases where the other person is so submissive that he is subject to domination by a would-be controller. While this may have the appearance of control, we believe that it fits more comfortably in the section on either power or influence. Understand also that this type of situation does not occur in healthy people. Healthy people reject attempts at manipulations they do not see in their own best interest.

There are probably a lot of ways this person can be seen and categorized. Three seem common enough to explore here.

The Compulsive Person

The compulsive person just never lets up. This woman always seems in a hurry. She is always busy and may be a workaholic. She just does not have time to smile or have fun. It is really sad to watch such a person. She is so intent on what she is doing she really does not have time to see or enjoy where she is.

This is generally the woman who believes that she is in control. Her inner feelings of exerting her will on the world have taken the form of a perpetual motion machine. Her greatest fear is that somehow the machine may run down. As long as it is still going, the illusion is safe. She does not really have time to properly assess the results. It is like the difference in business between cash flow and profits. You can look upon this woman as a cash machine, but not one who understands the bottom line. She simply keeps moving because, if she slows down, reality may set in. She may find that all of her beliefs about herself and her importance were largely in her own imagination.

In an organization, you can find this person fairly easily. She spends long, long hours at work. She is constantly on the move — reports, meetings, telephone calls, letters, etc. She generates a ton of paperwork, especially memos. Memos show everyone how much she is doing, how indispensable she is. Reading and answering them, of course, only slows things down.

When employees are asked for a job description, hers will invariably be the longest. This is a demonstration of how important she is. She will look like a model employee — industrious, loyal, dedicated. Chances are that if you look behind all the dust she has stirred up, you will find that she gets very little done . . . very little bottom line. She is so intent on action that she lacks any real organization. She is pointed so much towards the future that she has little real energy for substantive problems today.

It is really terrible when this person is the boss. She will expect everyone else to follow her lead. There will often be a game of who arrives first and leaves last. This is the person who has an absolute gift for getting into subordinates' areas, stirring up the pot, leaving without any conclusions, and then wondering aloud why everything is not okay.

One weapon in her arsenal that is particularly effective is the memo, and she uses it skillfully. She may also show martyr tendencies when she feels especially put upon, when she sighs and says it looks like she has just got to be responsible for everything. Control is essential.

Example. Marilyn had been with the company for about ten years. She had come out of college with a business degree and had worked her way up to an executive position with about fifty people reporting to her. She had always been looked upon as a great employee, very dedicated, hardworking, winning all of those other platitudes one often hears. She always went beyond the call of duty. When Marilyn arrived in the executive suite, her real self began to surface. Although she had always come in early and left late, she now began to prowl the halls to see who else was there with her. This caused a lot of anxiety among her employees. For those who might be healthy enough not to fall into the trap, she sent memos, memos, and more memos. They would always be time-dated, for example "7:00 A.M.," and would say things such as "When I was looking for you earlier . . . ," or "When I was in Saturday. . . . " This was bad enough, but her other favorite trick was to work an end run on the organizational chart, bypassing intermediate supervisors and going straight to lower level employees. She would talk over their "problems" with them and then retire to the safety of the carpeted area again. People would not know what to do or who was giving orders; havoc would ensue, and then she would tell her supervisors in their meetings that she just could not understand why they had such problems in their areas, usually ending with some comment about having to do everything herself. The games became a source of real irritation among employees. They were constantly confused about what was really going on. On the one hand they liked the close contact with the "boss" but on the other were also intimidated by it. All this time Marilyn thought she was doing a great job, keeping her finger on the pulse of what was happening in her area. While she was merely one of many employees, her controlling tendencies were sometimes an inconvenience; when she was an executive, they had a dramatically negative effect on the business.

The Martyr

This person may present one of two different faces. He may come across as put upon, overworked, excessively loyal — a real company man in the truest and worst sense. Or he may be the angry man, always in search of a new cause to champion. We will label these people as the *passive* martyr and the *aggressive* martyr.

The passive martyr is usually quiet, content to stay absorbed in her work. Her life seems to be one long series of sighs. If asked, she will tell you how she is working hard, constantly overloaded. Everyone is relying on her to come through. Without her, a lot of work just would not get done. She comes in early, leaves late, takes a big briefcase or two home, and is back on weekends. We once learned that this person in one office used a satchel to carry diet food from home each day. So much for image! Nonetheless, she gives the impression of diligence and differs from the compulsive person in that her compulsion is much quieter.

This employee tries to control the organization through her passivity. She leaves trails in the office that say "we can't get along without good ol' Judy. If you really need something done, give it to her and forget about it." She is not a particularly bad employee. She does in fact get a lot of work done, although she will appear to do more than she actually accomplishes. She is usually just plain boring. She is not likely to get really fired up, but she probably will not cause any real problems either. Several years ago the chairman of a major bank said words to the effect that "banking is the place where a well turned-out, presentable individual with a reasonably good education can find a life of quiet, dignified work. Our job is to identify these people and avoid hiring them." This may seem to be somewhat of an overstatement but does represent the thinking in at least one very large institution. In psychological terms, this person would probably be described as passive-aggressive. Her lack of a definitive emotional response to others becomes the method by which she tries to control them.

> *Example.* Margaret had been with the company for fifteen years. She was not really a barn burner when it came to work, but she was reliable and safe — someone who was always there and would not create any major problems. She looked like she got a lot of work done, but much of it was really paper shuffling. Over time, largely through attrition, she moved up the ladder. It was not so much that she was overly competent, but rather that she was there, very loyal. Management probably moved her along largely out of a sense of obligation. Then one day there was a major problem in the company, and lots of heads rolled. When it was all over, Margaret emerged as the senior person. Management saw her as a safe harbor in a storm, and so Margaret became president. She took all of her passive-aggressive qualities with her into this new position. When she was more or less buried in the organization, the problem was not so noticeable and certainly not overwhelming. But as a senior executive she was impossible. Margaret's long suit had never been truly listening or accepting advice from others. She always appeared attentive, seemed to take it all in, and then did whatever she had planned in the first place. This became a major problem for the company. Margaret refused to accept any input from other officers or from the board. She felt she was right and proceeded to exercise her unique brand of control through simply ignoring others. Margaret was slowly but systematically stripped of her authority. A new executive vice-president was brought in and slowly eased into the role of operating the business. Margaret was then promoted up into oblivion. She continued to be such a disruptive influence that finally she was retired, a polite term in this case for being fired.

On the other hand, the aggressive martyr is highly visible. He is always on the prowl, looking for a cause. You will be able to identify this person pretty easily. He is usually arrogant and always gets his nose in almost everything that does not concern him. He is the office rabble-rouser. Incidentally, we have also found this species on the college campus. He is the one who always wants to be at the center of what he sees as a power circle. If there is not a problem, he creates one. If he wrote as much as he talked, he would be the most published professor in the country.

This person may be somewhat productive in his work, but he would gladly rather be in the middle of some controversy. He deals in gossip and is an essential link in the company grapevine. He receives gossip and passes it on with his own colorful interpretations. If you want help in identifying this person, make up some story that is totally outrageous. Tell him in confidence. Then see how long it takes for the story to circulate. When you are new to an organization, this is not a bad way of getting the lay of the land.

Not only does he become involved in conflict, he loves to bring others into it. He "talks up" problems in the office after hours and tries to create an atmosphere that can only be described as confusion. His efforts to control vent themselves in creating or perpetuating adversity. This person is often seen buttonholing colleagues, whispering confidences, spending inordinate hours on the telephone, gathering allies, and wanting to talk to management about "the problem."

One of the interesting aspects of all this is that underneath all that bravado and bluster, he is usually a coward. If he is backed into a corner, he will surrender. His cause is not really so important that he is willing to sacrifice all for it. He will find that he just did not have all the facts, that a nameless "they" misled him, or that it is just not as important now as his new project. Both of these people live in their own worlds of self-constructed importance, one that is premised upon the idea that through this behavior comes a degree of control, one which, sadly enough, does not even exist.

Example. Sam had been in the company about three years before his basic character began to emerge. He had worked at his job pretty well and was considered a good although not brilliant employee. In his third year he was elected to an office in the employees' association, and he was off like a horse out of the gate. Instead of work, which was now performed minimally, he was caught up in looking for causes to champion. One that was of particular interest was the quality of the food in the company cafeteria. He decided that it was submarginal and spent most of his time trying to convince others of this. In addition, he approached senior management, demanding a meeting "on behalf of the employees' association." Interestingly, most people thought that the food, which was priced below comparable servings in restaurants, was pretty good, albeit institutionally routine. But this had become his platform. When confronted, Sam said that he was simply reflecting the wishes of concerned employees, nameless of course, who had approached him. And then he was off to a new cause. This probably would not be so bad except Sam stuck around for what seemed to management to be forever, always with a new banner to carry. The employees tended to vote him back into office since he was so highly visible, not necessarily effective, and because nobody else really wanted his slot in the employees' association. Sam saw himself as exerting great influence and control over the direction of the company. He thrived on crises. He believed the way to make his mark was to champion some cause.

The Inflated Person

This is often the office politician. This person spends a lot more time talking than working. He is the star of meetings, coffee breaks, lunches, after-work cocktails, and the telephone. Most of his energy goes into convincing himself just how important he really is. He sees himself as having a great deal of influence over the direction of the organization, his own unique brand of control. He also may have some of the characteristics of the aggressive martyr, but usually is a lot smoother and not totally keyed to dealing in adversity.

While he wants to be everybody's good friend, this person's ultra ego projects him as pompous. He likes to start conversations with things like "I've been meaning to get with you about. . . . " He tries to treat others as important confidantes and trades on "inside" information, somehow distinguishable in his mind from gossip. This "inside" position is one of his bases for control. Much of his energy is concentrated with trying to pry such information from others. He's also great at name-dropping. Conversations have phrases such as "I was talking to Sara [the president of the company] just the other day and she said . . . ," or "Sara was asking me about that recently and I told her. . . . " This reflected glory he experiences allows him to believe that others believe somehow he is truly on the inside.

Interestingly, a lot of co-workers will be fooled by him and buy into this behavior, largely because they also want to be on the inside track. Even secondhand information is prized. We have seen this where a small, loyal band is formed, and you can always expect that this coterie will be lined up in a wedge behind their leader. After a while it gets to be so predictable that it becomes the company joke.

If the inflated person is confronted about this problem, typically he retreats into one of two behaviors. The knowing smirk is always a good defense. It says that "if you knew what I know, you would never make that statement." This works pretty well with a lot of challengers. It creates enough doubt and fear that they will back off. The second technique is loud, aggressive bluster. Most civilized people choose not to be in a shouting match with a fool. So when confronted with a loud, angry, profane colleague, they will usually retire from the battlefield. So again the inflated person is protected within his own little dream world.

> **Example.** We think about one person, now dead, who had this down to a fine art. This person was a promoter, and when he had gotten past the point of sweet-talking, at which he was very good, he would shout, scream, cuss, and threaten. It is not too different from the high-pressure sales techniques where the salesperson tries to get you so angry through intimidation or guilt that you buy. The arguments this person made when he was turned down really did not make any sense. At the time, our comment was that he was a lot like a steamroller, trying to keep moving forward in an attempt to wear you down and roll over you. There was nothing subtle about what he did. It was an attempt at gross intimidation. We have to confess at that time to submitting to him sometimes, often getting extremely angry at him. There were times when it was easier simply to give in. That, of course, was his goal. Hopefully, we are better now.

POWER

Power can be defined as the attempt by one person to manipulate another person or his own environment either through agreement or the use of overt or covert threats. Power is an extremely effective motivator. It is what exists beyond or in place of money in the business world. It is what many people strive for. It is an alluring force that draws people into the upward spiral of a business organization. When a person has enough money to be comfortable, what he then seeks is power.

Unlike control, power is real. It allows the holder to truly change things. It exists in the context of relationships. Here both parties are aware of its existence. They have positioned themselves where such power is explicitly or implicitly agreed upon or tacitly understood. This is the bedrock for all employer-employee relationships.

Unlike control, where the controller seeks unilaterally to impose his will on others, power emanates from a relationship that is essentially bilateral, not unlike a contract between two people. Both have voluntarily placed themselves in their respective positions. Both have the ability to change this by moving away from the relationship. It may be said that some people are locked into their jobs. While this may appear to be true, ultimately they have the freedom of choice about their affiliation. Thus, power is based upon a consensual relationship, one wherein the consent is continuous, albeit at times reluctant.

The question of legitimacy is important when speaking of power, as it can be exercised toward either legitimate or illegitimate ends. When a person talks about the legitimate exercise of power, he thinks of the exchange between people taking a form which was either explicitly agreed upon, implicitly understood, or was foreseeable in terms of the relationship. In short, there are no real surprises.

Between employer and employee, it is acknowledged that certain conditions of employment, such as hours, wages, working space, and other requirements, are to be set, subject in some cases to union demands, by the employer. To this extent, the employer exercises legitimate power over the employee. Circumstances may change, and these may dictate changes in the conditions of employment. This should be understood by any reasonable person entering into employment.

Where, then, does illegitimate exercise of power arise? It occurs when something outside the "contractual" conditions between employer and employee transpires. For example, if a condition of continued employment requires the exchange of sexual favors or the commission of a criminal act, the employer has abused power. What happens in this latter case to the employee? He has several choices. First, he may simply choose to walk away from the job. However, financial necessity may militate against this. He may simply submit, which, while a viable alternative, may not be the best solution. He may try to negotiate with the boss. Or he may try to modify the relationship to accommodate to the changes.

In any event, power is very real, often the most definitive and visible characteristic between people in business. Its effects have far-ranging consequences within the relationship. It is a common element in business, and without it there would be a good chance of anarchy and chaos. Properly used, power results in production. To illustrate the use of power, we are going to examine two different people to show a contrast in how the mantle of power is worn and how it is exercised.

Example. Robert had been successful in his chosen line of work. Coming from near poverty, he had obtained an outstanding education, proceeding through the graduate school of a prestigious Ivy League college. His climb up the corporate ladder had been marked by one success after another. Robert had come to his present company as president. There were no major problems the former CEO had merely retired, and the board reached outside for his replacement. The business employed a relatively small but extremely competent, professional staff and was largely geared to interacting with the public. It's questionable whether Robert had a solid idea of the concept of power, or whether he constantly confused it with control. Nevertheless, he immediately set about establishing his base and territory with both his board and with his customers. While he gave lip service to the importance of his employees, it was apparent from the outset that they were to play a fully supporting role to the star and that both they and their needs were unimportant beyond that. And Robert really worked hard at being the star. He dressed in the best that Brooks Brothers had to offer (living in the Southwest at a time when Brooks had stores only in New York and Chicago), wore hand-tooled shoes, drove a very expensive car, lived in the "right" neighborhood (old but very proper), and belonged to the right clubs. Robert's life was largely a piece of cardboard, a facade he had erected to support his own failing self-image. He looked to his staff to help maintain this illusion. Life in business with Robert was always tumultuous. He kept his employees off balance constantly with his incessant and often conflicting demands. He ruled largely through intimidation. There was always the threat of being fired. Because the organization was small, no one, not even custodians, escaped his notice. The most striking thing about Robert's management style and his use of power was that, while he set very high standards for his employees, he had very low expectations — an important point. He actually expected people to fail. And then he would have to come in, world weary with all of his burdens, and pick up the pieces. This is how he tried to control things.

Example. On the other hand, Mike came from an upper middle-class family background. He was born to be in business. His state university education gave him some tools to use, but he succeeded largely on an almost inborn business instinct. Mike was also interested in the trappings of success and enjoyed many of the same kinds of things Robert did. However, for some reason, it seemed to fit more comfortably with him . . . like he was not trying so hard to make an appearance, more just to be comfortable. Mike built up his own business, expanded, and diversified. As he did this, he brought a number of other people along with him. There was absolutely no question in anyone's mind about who was boss in this organization. Everyone deferred to Mike. But this was so natural no one seemed concerned or, for that matter, really aware of it.

Where is the difference? Mike worked hard and earned his own way in the company. Robert went through a lot of motions but was more interested in his image than in real work. Mike set high goals for his people and, unlike Robert, fully expected them to perform at that level. He tried to equip his employees with the necessary tools and gave them his full support. He did not see himself as the sole star of the production and was willing to share or even step aside and allow others to enjoy the glory when they had earned it.

In the first case, power bordering on control was used to coerce and intimidate employees into submission. They were constantly living on the edge. In the second case, power was never really brought to bear inside the company, rather just accepted. The real effort was made toward the customer. A lot had to do with individual style. Robert had to be constantly reassured that he was in charge and that everyone was working for him. Mike was comfortable with himself and so clearly defined in his role and relationship in the business that he did not need to fight constantly for it.

SELF-DISCIPLINE

Self-discipline is learning to identify, choose, and limit his responses to his own emotions, other people, and outside events in his life. The word *discipline* is used here in the context of self-discipline rather than meaning punishment of some sort.

People often talk about "bad feelings" as though emotions had some value. We believe that human emotions are neutral, that is, there is no value that can be assigned to them. Feelings simply happen. People generally do not program and call up feelings. When certain things happen in their lives, they feel certain ways. And they have no "control" over these feelings. (We recognize that there are psychologists and perhaps others who will disagree with this proposition. We do have some company in our beliefs about the neutrality of feelings. Eunice Cavanaugh points out in her book *Understanding Shame* that "Feelings are neither 'good' or 'bad.' Feelings just are. To label them can be confusing and crazy-making" [1989, p. 12]. And in *Co-dependent No More*, Melody Beattie points out that "Feelings are not wrong. They're not inappropriate. We don't need to feel guilty about feelings. Feelings are not acts. . . . Feelings shouldn't be judged as either good or bad. Feelings are emotional energy; they are not personality traits" [1987, p. 133].)

How people respond to feelings definitely does have value. They have the ability to limit their responses to those feelings. This is a learned behavior. As young children they tended to react to feelings in ways that would be wholly inappropriate for adults. An angry child may well hit the other person. An adult hopefully can respond in some other way. The feeling or emotion is the same. Over the years people have learned responses other than simply striking out.

Some people will want to call this response "control." There is no real quarrel over the semantics so long as the nature of the response is understood. This is not "control" in the sense that a person can simply exercise his willpower over his emotions, but rather that he has learned how to react to those emotions in ways that are more socially acceptable. And so when the feeling occurs, he chooses a response from his repertoire that is appropriate to his age and the circumstances. These responses are reality based and represent a mature way of dealing with ourselves, others, and our environment. The responses that are made serve a legitimate purpose and allow healthy, mature transactions to take place between people in a relationship.

Example. One of the most interesting places we have seen this in action is in the banking industry. We have watched the reactions of two different loan officers to the same stimulus: a customer who was unable to repay his or her loan as agreed. Terry always sat down with the customer and tried to work out a solution that was reasonable and would allow the bank to eventually get its money repaid. Frank, on the other hand, almost always became angry and felt as though the customer had insulted him. He treated the money as though it were his own and seemed to feel that the customer had purposely arranged his finances so the bank would not be repaid. Frank would be in a terrible mood all day and would end up treating other customers badly, often turning down credit-worthy customers while he was in this bad mood. In one extreme case we saw Frank actually drive a customer into bankruptcy out of anger and spite. As a result the bank did not get anything.

Here were two people working in the same type of business who had very similar experiences. They chose very different responses to the events in their business lives. One acted reasonably while the other became angry. Same stimulus, different responses. We do this as individuals also. We may take very similar events and react very differently, depending upon a number of other factors. The "feeling" we receive is neither "good" nor "bad." It just is. But our choice of response is all-critical.

INFLUENCE

The final transaction we will discuss is influence. *Influence* is defined as the ability of one person through the use of reason, logic, or personal qualities to persuade another to change his position or belief voluntarily.

With influence, one person makes his best case for change and leaves the choice up to the other person. Influence may be felt at different levels, ranging from the very conscious to the unconscious. It is based upon the reality of the circumstances, alternatives, and probable outcomes as perceived by both parties. Here the first party subscribes to a particular belief or course of action and is able to persuade the other party to adopt this position.

Reason and logic may be determinative. The argument that has been made is simply too powerful and compelling to ignore. Quite often the personal qualities of the persuader are important. Chief among these is credibility, which comes about through past relationships, experiences, or knowledge. Second, the persuader is usually required to be sincere as he approaches the person to be swayed. Third, the circumstances must be timely, the information needed for decisions in the present or near future. Finally, the data must be useful, proximately connected to the problem to be solved.

So if we are able to supply you with the right information at the right time, appear interested and concerned about you in these circumstances, and have some standing with you through past associations or experience, you may be likely to accept our position. In some cases eloquence is helpful, but this generally ranks behind these other qualities with a healthy person.

How do people react? A truly perceptive person will carefully weigh the information he has received, will accept what is useful and reject that which does not fit or is uncomfortable, will make a decision, and will act. The co-dependent will tend to take in everything he hears and make it his own. To the extent that there are conflicting views presented to him, he will tend to accept and go with the ideas and thoughts of the last person he encounters. This is one reason, for example, that in union elections management is muzzled for the twenty-four-hour period prior to the election.

In some cases the attempt to influence is legitimate and serves a useful purpose. In others, it can be useful, but there is a chance of abuse. To the extent influence is abused, its goals are at least suspect. Propaganda and demagoguery fall into this latter category.

Influence is extremely important in the world of business. It is the way that most business transactions occur, certainly among equals. It is the basis for negotiating. Without the process of give and take, business would quickly grind to a halt.

The ability to persuade people is a hallmark of leadership. It is more effective in the long run than power-based relationships. We look back and try to catalogue the qualities we've seen and heard about from others about influential people. Without trying to sound like a manual on leadership, we want to share some of the ones we believe are most important. Charlotte, a composite person, is real in the sense that people really do have these qualities.

Example. To begin with, Charlotte is competent. This is probably the most important quality she has to offer. She knows her job and works hard at it. She has realistic expectations for herself as well as those who work for her. Generally, her employees help set their goals with her once annually. Then she helps and encourages them in attaining those goals. Charlotte is fair in the sense that she does not try to be sneaky or to blind-side employees. She is very open about the business, and everyone knows where she stands. She is quick to praise and compliment her employees, but not reticent about criticizing them when necessary. They feel as though they understand her and know what is going on in the business. With Charlotte, if you do less than your best, you feel as though you have let her down. She has never said anything to bring on this feeling — it is just there. In a meeting a few years ago, the CEO of a company asked some assembled employees to define a leader. One person answered that "A leader is a person who has followers." Charlotte qualifies. And as such, she is enormously persuasive when she tries to sell an idea. People tend to believe that if she supports it, it must be okay.

We would like to suggest that the person who is most likely to be successful in business is one who has achieved some social and psychological maturity. This person recognizes that he is in fact not able to "control" life. His own emotions, other people, institutions, and events in his life are simply realities to be considered and dealt with. He knows that if he attempts to exert his will over them, he is dissipating his supply of energy. And as he does this, he will experience frustration and failure. Further, it leaves him a reduced amount of energy to deal with the real world and, thus, lessens his likelihood of success.

He also knows that power is very real, having probably experienced it from both sides. As he matures, he also sees power as a legitimate method of dealing with some issues. Certainly, organizational structure and day-to-day operations can take place simply because it is policy, i.e., the boss says so. Generally, no one will seriously dispute this.

Power does have its limitations. To the extent the boss wants to move his employee in a direction the latter resists, and if that resistance becomes entrenched, power resolves itself to an either/or conclusion. This may result in a lose-lose situation, both parties failing to get what they want or need.

Effective managers recognize that power distilled down to force is self-limiting. Likewise, unused power tends to be more awesome since the recipient does not know its exact extent, or how vigorously the possessor will be using it. Once it is used, it is known and can be assessed for future situations. The greatest power is the unused power.

Next, he understands that he has a range of responses to given stimuli. Over time he will learn which of those best serve him in business situations. He is able to choose responses that are appropriate for the conditions and circumstances. Through self-discipline he hopefully is able to invoke positive responses.

The stage is now set to allow this person to attempt to motivate others through persuasion, to influence other people to follow a course of action. This is the most mature way of managing people, one where the influenced person feels and believes that he indeed has some choices in his own destiny.

CHAPTER 9

BUSINESS AS A SYSTEM

The late Virginia Satir had a great technique for demonstrating some of the dynamics of a system. She would take a family and connect each of the members to one another with short pieces of rope tied around their waists. She would place them in a circle and have them be quiet. Then she had them imagine the phone was ringing and the oldest child getting up to answer it, or the mother needing to go to the kitchen, or the father wanting to take a walk. We all go through life with a lot of invisible strings attached to us, and if there is movement we are pulled or jerked in some direction (Satir, 1972, pp. 158 et seq.).

From this simple exercise she was able to demonstrate how each family member was affected by the actions of others as well as by outside forces. John Bradshaw does essentially the same thing today on public television with a mobile. This is a good starting place for us to discuss systems.

In looking at problems related to any business, it seems appropriate to take the time to discuss business as a system. This will help us understand how businesses exist in the context of other systems rather than in a vacuum. This chapter will tend to be a little more academic in presentation. We have tried to make this understandable for the reader since our stated purpose is to reach as many people as possible in a practical manner.

Augustus Napier and Carl Whitaker have taken a general systems approach to exploring family dynamics in *The Family Crucible* (1978). We want to acknowledge their work because it has provided us with a basis for using a systemic approach to the current problem. And so by interpretation and extrapolation, we will attempt to apply many of their ideas here.

> *Example.* If we try to define a system in a business sense, we might look at a typical office in an organization. There are six people working here under one manager. Their job is to maintain accounts payable. Each person within the office has a well-defined role, certain responsibilities he or she is supposed to perform. Each one works separately in his or her designated area. They receive input from all over the business as accounts payable are contracted. Their work goes together to form the whole area of accounts payable. This in turn becomes a part of the general accounting function of the company. So what has happened is that we have individuals working and interacting with one another in a group setting. But what they do is affected by others outside who are constantly feeding data to them, and what they do affects others outside who are receiving information from them. This is a system at work as well as a unit within a larger system. Each affects and is affected by others. None exists in isolation.

The thrust of a general systems theory is that things neither happen by accident nor do they exist in isolation. At whatever level we view life and our environment, there seems to be a definable, more or less orderly pattern in which everything co-exists in relationship to other things. What this theory does is to allow us to look at very complex parts of our existence and to conceptualize them in a way in which we can ascertain and define the factors common to all of them. Systems are of two general types: living and nonliving. However, even though we separate these for convenience, they nonetheless still interact with one another, and both have an impact on persons who live within them.

Systems are organized in such a way that they can give definition and meaning to us in life. They allow us to sense some balance and consistency in what goes on within and around us, and perhaps, at times, even have some predictability. There are boundaries in a system, and we can more easily see one object or event in terms of its relationship to others. These relationships occur both within the primary system where the event is taking place and in a variety of secondary systems where the event touches upon other events or objects.

Systems seek to maintain themselves, that is, they are homeostatic. Within its boundaries, a system resists outside influences and change. (Each of us can look to our own families to see how resistive we are to any radical changes within our family unit.) When it does in fact change, it can do so either voluntarily or involuntarily. When the system voluntarily changes, it does so based upon information concerning its environment. We see feedback — getting information back about behavior — as one technique that helps accomplish this. It is as though a radar beam is transmitted outward, and when it returns, the information that the image projects provides the system with the necessary information to make a decision to change its character, goals, and direction. Living systems perform this activity as a natural part by their own volition.

An involuntary shift may occur within a system when outside events are so compelling that there are no viable alternatives to change. Such changes may be temporary where the system seeks to elude or escape something that threatens its comfort, safety, or existence, or these changes may be permanent when the outside event itself has become a new, fixed reality.

It is important to see a particular system in the context of its total existence. Many parts, other systems, come together to form a new system at a given place and time. In turn, this system then coalesces with other systems to form a new, larger one. Systems are ranked hierarchically. They begin in existence with the atomic particle and move upwards to a community of nations. Napier and Whitaker have suggested the following ranking, in ascending order:

Atom particle
atom
molecule
organ
organ systems

Person or Organism
nuclear family
extended family
community subgroup (work, friendship)
city or community
county
state
nation
national alliance
whole community of nations (1978, p. 49–50).*

In this hierarchy, for example, each of us fits as an individual. We are a part of a chain that trails downward and extends upward from us. Generally, larger systems tend to have some power or influence over smaller ones, thus allowing the larger systems to direct events downward. Influence, on the other hand, may move up or down the ladder. Thus, when we begin to look at human behavior, at any level, we must understand that it is not a two-dimensional event but requires the integration of information and knowledge from many different levels.

People are affected not only by a hierarchical chain such as we have described. At any given level there are many systems and subsystems working. For example, to take a simpler situation structurally, within a nuclear family there are a number of possible combinations that may exist at any given time.

> If we have a husband (H), wife (W), boy child (B), and girl child (G), consider that we may have the following dyads:
>
>   HW   HB   HG   WB   WG   BG
> or triads:
>   BWG   HWG   HGB   HWB
> or as a family:
>   HWBG

All eleven of these combinations must be considered since differing combinations at different times produce different behavioral results. We, at this point, are looking only within the nuclear family itself. This family, in turn, is influenced by other levels in its hierarchical chain. This is not simple. Family members move off in different directions as they move up the ladder, e.g., school, work, clubs, social activities, etc. Sometimes they go their separate ways, and at other times they may move in groups of some sort. H and B may go to Boy Scouts, W and G to Girl Scouts, H and W to P.T.A., B and G to school, etc. Every place family members go, they contact some other system that ultimately affects them as individuals.

People learn a great deal in the nuclear family. They also learn from

---

*Used with permission, Augustus Napier and Carl Whitaker (1978).
The Family Crucible. New York: Harper & Row Publishers.

others with whom they have contact. Transcending this direct learning is the fact that they learn from their environment and the social networks that surround them. Finally, if you subscribe to a type of Jungian idea of the collective unconscious, they are born with a certain knowledge acquired from the ages. So at any given point in time in our lives, our individual histories, we are the product of hereditary subsystems, the system in which we live with all its permutations, other systems that may be peripheral but nonetheless exert and influence us, as well as the environment and social structure surrounding us.

Consider also that when one part, just one single part, of an influencing system is altered, the system itself changes. These changes may be almost imperceptible, or they may be cataclysmic, but they are changes. Thus, we are always changing, never exactly the same through time.

What we have looked at here is a family and the individuals within that family. Consider then how much more complex a business organization can be. We take everything we have looked at so far with, say, 7,000 people, and then put them all together in yet another system. Each person brings along whatever has developed in the past.

A business develops its own systemic existence. Not only is it affected by all of the very complex component parts, but it has its own hierarchy and subsystems. In addition, it has a number of systems that are commonly called *stakeholders*, people and groups who have a real or imagined vested interest in what the business does. Some of these are primary, some secondary:

Primary	Secondary
Stockholders	Communities
Employees	Federal, state, local,
Customers	and foreign governments
Creditors	Business support groups
Suppliers	Social/activist groups
Wholesaler, retailer	Media
Competitors	General public

The whole idea of a general systems theory is exciting; it draws upon a number of different disciplines and backgrounds. There is a tendency to unify existence by showing us where our interests converge. This may represent an ultimate interrelationship among all things in life.

Systems may also create confusion. If this approach is correct, how can we ever sort out everything in a way that makes some sense? First, we may see the individual as the basic unit in the hierarchy. This is not because of some mystical quality the individual possesses; rather it is because that is what we are and what we can best see, examine, and understand. Second, when we look at a system, and in our case a business as a system, there are certain properties that systems tend to have in common. So we can focus our attention on these:

Organization
> How the system is organized.

Information
> Process — how the system receives and processes information.
> Utilization — how the system actually uses information.
> Communication — how the system communicates the
>> information.

Interactions
> Internal — how people within the system carry out daily
>> functions.
> External — how the system relates to outsiders.
> Change — how the system goes about changing.

It is easier to work with an individual, and it makes more sense to see what is happening between people. When we shift from the individual to some group or organization, the question arises of what to do with the individual. The easiest thing to do is to put some type of a label on him and tuck him neatly away in a pigeonhole.

People who are so labeled tend to be carriers of any type of disorder that affects the system as a whole. Some acts taken by the system are very positive, while others can have negative effects. For example, any organization, like humans, may engage in denial, control, perfectionism, and blame, and is generally disturbed if it learns that it is somehow responsible for its own problems.

So when we look at an organization, it seems appropriate to look at all of the forces, both positive and negative, that affect the individual within that system and from that try to learn whether the system attempts to promote healthy growth and what changes, if any, within the system are indicated.

This is a very brief overview of systems and their applications to business organizations. This chapter is not meant to be exhaustive, rather to help the reader see how complex things become when one tries to examine a large organization. It also points to the fact that businesses, like humans, do not live in isolation, but are always affected by events around them. Finally, co-dependency itself has to exist in terms of interrelationships and must be approached and studied in those terms.

CHAPTER 10

RECOVERY

A lot of what we read today about co-dependency deals with problems stemming from it, both in business and in other areas. Some writers have discussed how to deal with co-dependency, especially on a personal level. We have not found anything significant, however, which talks about the problem of or recovery from what we have called organizational co-dependence.

In the beginning, when researchers were just starting to look at organizational co-dependency, it was inappropriate to look for solutions since the problem had never been clearly defined. But we have moved further along in our exploration of organizational co-dependency, and, thus, we believe we should now be looking at solutions to the problem. And there are some steps anyone can take that will start this recovery process.

When we talk about recovery, it is not to suggest that something will happen one day that will magically cure these problems. We are talking about a process of trying to learn to survive in a world filled with co-dependent people. You may or may not fit the descriptions we have included or that you have read somewhere else, that personally you are or are not co-dependent. Whether or not you are personally co-dependent, in this world you need to deal with people who have this disease, and how you prepare for this is important. If you venture into battle without your armor, you run the risk of becoming a casualty.

We have explored the problem of co-dependency in an organizational setting from three general perspectives:
1. co-dependency a person has before entering the organization (personal co-dependency)

2. co-dependency a person acquires as a result of contacts with the organization (organizational co-dependency)
3. organizational behaviors that create, perpetuate, and exacerbate co-dependency

As we look at solutions, what we term recovery in a broad sense, we will use these same three categories.

PERSONAL CO-DEPENDENCY

Again, this type of co-dependency originates sometime before the person comes to the organization. It may be primary where the onset is during childhood, or it may be secondary where it begins during adult life. Treatment for these two types is different. With primary co-dependency the focus is on childhood and family-of-origin issues, while help for the secondary type addresses detachment.

It is not our purpose here to explore all of the techniques used to facilitate individual recovery. This has been done very well by numerous writers including, among others, Beattie, Bradshaw, Cermak, and Wegscheider-Cruse. We do want to make some observations about how affected employees deal with this problem in their employment. We have written about this area previously and offer it again here (Goff and Goff, 1988, pp. 56–57).

Do Nothing

For many people the best solution is to do nothing. It should be noted that this is not only a realistic solution to the problem, but one that will be chosen by many people. A system has been created in which the employee and the employer are members. Like other systems there will be resistance to change. It may be "bad," but it is predictable (even in its own unpredictability). The employee continues to work, anxiously waiting to see what each day will bring, but somehow develops enough survival skills to make it through the day and continue to work.

Leave the Job

The employee may just walk off the job. There are many other issues that interplay with this decision, such as financial ability to quit or another job waiting. The real problem is that by the time the employee decides to leave this job situation, he is likely to have become so immersed in his own co-dependent behavior that he simply carries these traits to another job.

108

When the move is made, chances are good the employee will find another uncomfortable situation. People tend to unconsciously seek the type of relationships they need. A co-dependent needs someone to fix; therefore, the next time, the employee may find a boss who is addicted to something, or an organization where co-dependent qualities will be welcomed. The process will usually repeat itself without any awareness on the employee's part.

Seek Help

The fortunate few find help. It is a sad fact that most people drift through life without understanding why they are having problems at work and why they are unhappy. They never realize there are choices available to them. Therefore, they spend most of their time and energy thinking about how things might have been different or how they may be different in the future. Life for such individuals becomes a series of memories and dreams, but no present reality. They spend so much energy in the past and the future that they have little left to focus on a full and happy life today.

How does this person become so fortunate to know to seek help? Usually it takes a life crisis. This crisis may be a giant event, or it may be an accumulation of smaller, but combined, incidents. Often the situation occurs in relationships outside work. The problems on the outside force the employee to seek some type of help. This may happen through an employee assistance program, private counseling, or by means of some self-help group like Al-Anon or Adult Children of Alcoholics.

Once co-dependency is recognized, it can be treated, or at least dealt with, by the person having to work with an affected individual. Essentially, treatment starts when the co-dependent stops trying to take care of others and be responsible for everyone else and learns to love and care for himself.

Recovery consists of learning and practicing new and different behaviors. Among them are:

- Understanding co-dependency
- Accepting it
- Not trying to control others
- Not accepting responsibility for another person's behavior
- Dealing with anger

- Detachment
- Caring for oneself first

Again, these have all been explored in more detail by other writers, and we recommend their works to you. This is meant to be a very broad overview of the problem and solutions in this one particular area.

ORGANIZATIONAL CO-DEPENDENCY

The focus of this section is how a person within an organization can protect himself against organizational behaviors that may cause co-dependency. We believe this falls into three general categories: (1) self-knowledge, (2) knowledge of the corporate style, and (3) retaining a personal identity.

Self-Knowledge

Perhaps the most important element in self-defense is how well the person understands his own personality. If one truly understands and *accepts* who he is before he goes into the workplace, he has a sense of personal integrity about his own identity that will allow him to weather most of the storms he may encounter. Unfortunately, this description excludes vast numbers of workers. We find that many people, for a variety of reasons, have never had or taken the opportunity to examine their own lives and values and make some statement about who they really are. They go through life without ever knowing this. Some do very well with this and are reasonably happy without this knowledge. Others have a very difficult time.

Self-examination is especially important when the person looks at the possibility that he may already have some co-dependent patterns in his life. This alone takes a good bit of work and is not something one can determine by simply making a declaration about himself. It is important to know this since a person who enters an organization while he is truly healthy has a good chance of escaping the co-dependence trap while he is there. If he is unaware of himself as a person, he may be more vulnerable in an organizational setting. If he is truly free of co-dependency, then he can use some of the techniques that we explored in the preceding section to help ward off any corporate attitudes that might draw him closer to the brink of co-dependency.

Knowledge of the Corporate Style

The first rule in this category is to know and accept that some businesses have behaviors that may create co-dependency in their employees. Like individuals, most businesses will have some of these characteristics at least from time to time. The question is whether business has become so ingrained that it represents a management style the employee has to cope with, or whether management has either the insight or luck to move safely through these times into calmer waters.

Some company characteristics should serve as warning signals to the new employee. We mention a few of these here. Everyone who reads this can undoubtedly add to the list.

- Employees are supersensitive to the moods of the manager
- Fear among employees
- Abusive behavior by management
- An indifference by management to employee needs
- Harassment, sexual or otherwise
- Expectations employees will give unpaid overtime
- Rigid rules about terms of employment
- Company policies that invade employee privacy
- Poor communication patterns
- No sense of humor among employees and managers
- A fear of employee creativity
- No access by employees to managers

Second, the employee has to be careful not to be lured into the traps laid by co-dependency. Sometimes they are very seductive, especially to the newcomer. Co-dependency comes cleverly disguised as does true caring and concern for others. What begins as an innocent-appearing activity can balloon into full-blown co-dependency before the employee is released from its grip.

Newcomers are singled out because they are most susceptible to the allure of organizational co-dependency. (By this we do not mean to imply that "old-timers" are somehow exempt from this problem, merely that they do not have the same dynamics working on them as a person who has just come to work.) Newcomers may see what others are doing and, in their eagerness to fit in, be trapped into unhealthy patterns before they really recognize what has happened. It is much easier to stay out of this pit than to try to scale the walls out of it.

> *Example.* A new employee may be asked to pitch in and help a
> co-worker finish a job. This is normally not an unreasonable request,
> and most employees, new or otherwise, will try to be helpful. Coop-
> erating on the job helps everyone accomplish the work. This is,
> however, a favorite technique of a manager who has an alcoholic
> working for him and is afraid to address the problem. What he does
> is to ask others to take up the slack created by the addict's failure to
> perform. He may refuse to deal with the affected employee for a
> number of reasons, such as: he does not like confrontations; it will
> appear he cannot run his own area; the employee may get fired; he
> must address his own chemical use, etc. The point is that he is making
> other employees responsible — the caretakers — for the addict. This
> pattern can become a habit. It is classic co-dependency, a type that
> has been created by the organization.

Third, he can confront the issue. This may not be really popular
and may anger some people, especially managers who are accustomed
to a co-dependent style. But he can say that this behavior is not one
he wants to participate in and politely excuse himself from these
damaging activities. This could conceivably cost him his job. We
suggest, however, that it would be better to be out of work than to be
working in a place that was going to cause long-term problems in the
employee's life. It is much the same as a person's deciding not to stay
somewhere if there are physical safety hazards.

Some people may feel that this is somewhat of an overstatement.
We believe the risk to the individual is every bit as real in the case of
co-dependency as it would be with a safety hazard. The only difference
is the amount of time it takes for the problem to become acute: with
the safety hazard the problem is immediate while with co-dependency
it is deferred. Both can be hazardous, and both can become fatal.
Untreated co-dependence can, by definition, cause physical problems.

Retaining a Personal Identity

The sense of personal integrity one has is a good solid wall between
himself and co-dependency. If this is well developed, he can withstand
a lot of pressure. He is able to take care of himself. Organizations tend
to use the people who most allow themselves to be used. They trade on
the goodwill and corporate loyalty people have. It is important that he
not allow himself to be consumed by the organization. If he allows this,
the company will swallow him. As one observer noted, "They'll take

and suck you dry and then spit you out." This can be true, although every business does not do this same thing to the same extent. But nearly every organization will continue to intrude on the good nature of a willing employee as long as it can.

So it becomes important in the very beginning to establish boundaries between one's job and one's private life. Setting boundaries, of course, applies equally in interpersonal relationships. While we look at boundaries between people, we sometimes neglect to see the necessity for this in relationships with organizations. We think both are important. And if one is to preserve his own identity, he must set boundaries from the outset. This means making certain everyone understands that he does have interests outside the business and that it is his intent to continue to pursue them. Staking out and jealously guarding one's territory is the best defense against an overly intrusive organization.

With outside interest it seems important to make some friends outside the company. Too often, people — especially migrant executives — rely on the company for their social contacts. When this happens, people seem to make social events simply an extension of the office. This is fraught with a lot of inbreeding, which we believe is unhealthy for the company itself as well as for the employees who engage in it. It also tends to exclude family members, generally spouses, who are not on the inside and therefore really do not have a lot to say and do at these functions. Further, it tends to breed the hierarchical system into social occasions, something that must be contended with by both the employees and their partners.

This can be very unhealthy since there seems to be no relief from the pressures of work. If the organization has some of the characteristics that breed co-dependency, individuals have a greater opportunity to adopt a dependent life-style simply because they are exposed to it most of the time.

Conversely, when people reach outside their organizational structure for social contacts, they have a chance to be around different people whose values and life-styles may help promote more healthy growth. There is a constant infusion of fresh thought and conversation, something that is nearly impossible when the intracompany socializing mentioned above happens.

Beyond friends, employees should develop other interests outside the company. If a person wants to play softball, that is fine. But perhaps he could try out for a city league team instead of devoting all of his time to the company team. Golf or tennis are fine sports but can be pursued with people other than company friends or in the context of company tournaments.

Maintaining a personal life outside a company is very difficult at times. In some organizations, especially the ones that tend to promote more unhealthy life-styles, there may be a lot of pressure to keep everything "within the company family." An employee may find that he has to swim against the stream in order to survive. Survival may seem like a strong word to use; however, it fairly represents what is going on in this situation. As we mentioned before, this is an attempt by the employee to distance himself from a condition that is unsafe or unhealthy for him.

For an excellent example of this inward-directed social life, we turn to the military. Military installations are essentially closed communities. They do not encourage any cross-pollination with surrounding communities outside of the obligatory contacts senior ranking officers are expected to have with community leaders to promote goodwill. Most socialization occurs on-base and is structured around the table of organization. Even the informality of an officers' open mess is tainted with inbreeding. It takes on the characteristics of a caste system, with each officer knowing where he is in the pecking order.

Of course, the military demands loyalty and unquestioning responses to orders. There are some good reasons for this, especially in battle. If one is leading an infantry platoon into combat, he does not want a discussion about whether the unit should take the hill. Lives are at stake there. While carryovers into peacetime life are somewhat exaggerated, they are understandable.

Some corporations are nearly as rigid as the military. There is no overriding national interest in this posturing, but it has become more comfortable for the senior executives to mix with company people than with outsiders. They are able to get the homage they feel they are due in that setting. Employees, for their own mental health, should resist the efforts of an organization to push them into a corporate mold antagonistic to their sense of self-worth.

ORGANIZATIONAL BEHAVIORS

Dealing with the behaviors that tend to cause co-dependent problems means that an organization has to take a look into its own corporate soul. This process is often painful and may result in some changes within the company that are very uncomfortable for both management and employees. It may well mean that management styles will have to be reviewed and changed. Frankly, most companies are unwilling to make a commitment at this level.

We have looked at some of the problems attendant to changing any system. No matter how bad it may be, there is an investment by the members of that system in maintaining the status quo. The comfort that comes from the known is hard to fight. Therefore, in order for a company to change, it takes the commitment of senior management. Without this type of support, nothing constructive or lasting will happen.

Sadly, very few managers at that level have the knowledge, time, or inclination to address this problem. It is very hard to quantify the results in terms of money. Most managers use a utilitarian system — a cost-benefit analysis — to make strategic decisions about what is really important to the company. We cannot tell a manager that he will save X number of dollars if he can change certain behaviors. Yet, we know, perhaps intuitively, that monetary benefits can flow from looking at this just as surely as cash benefits flow from programs like employee assistance plans (Appendix C).

In order for management to deal effectively with this problem, we believe several things must happen. The organization should:

1. learn about co-dependency and accept it as a reality
2. determine if the company has the problem and, if so, the extent of it
3. address the specific behaviors that cause the problem:
    a. breaking the shame cycle
    b. impersonality
    c. hierarchy
    d. comparisons and competition
    e. poor communication patterns
    f. spiritual nature of human beings

Learn About Co-dependency and Accept It As a Reality

This is an educational process, one that may be done in-house if there is expertise, or one that can be done with outside consultants. Again, there are precious few people who truly understand this phenomenon, although many profess to have a real grasp of it from having read a book or two. Selection of a co-dependency expert is very important and will largely decide how effective the rest of the rehabilitation program will be. We suggest that managers interview applicants for this job very closely about their qualifications and whether they will know what to do in the event they find a co-dependent problem. You might want to begin by asking how they define co-dependency, something that can often be a timesaving tip-off.

Reading about co-dependency will help managers have a better understanding of some of its dynamics. By extrapolation, they can begin to see corporate behaviors that parallel those in interpersonal relations. This will lay some groundwork for a later look at the company. We feel that any accurate information the managers get will help. (A number of books on co-dependency are listed in the Reference and Suggested Reading sections. We feel that these are excellent and recommend any or all of them.)

Determine if the Company Has the Problem and, if so, the Extent of It

This ties directly into the first item on the agenda. When the initial study is being done, whoever the expert happens to be can make an assessment about whether this is even an issue and, if so, how deeply infected the company is with co-dependency. Again, remember that all companies will at times be symptomatic. The trick is to make certain to distinguish between these temporary problems and those that have become entrenched. This is done through interviews with key people in the organization, acquiring a sense of history and management style, and then interviewing enough line and staff employees to see what effects corporate behavior has had on them.

Particular attention needs to be paid to the specific behaviors we have discussed as well as any others that several employees see as being a problem within the organization. All of the negative behaviors do not have to be present in order for co-dependency to be fostered. One may be enough in some cases. Likewise there may be other dysfunctional behaviors we have chosen not to list but which may have their origins in co-dependent-type problems and may be affecting the company adversely. The question is not so much what is happening but rather how is it affecting the people within the company.

Address the Specific Behaviors That Cause the Problem

This can be done effectively in any number of ways, depending on the size and structure of the company. For example:

- We may hold a company meeting to discuss the problem and its solutions.
- We may hold a series of employee meetings where employees are given the opportunity to express their feelings.
- We may work through the organizational structure, allowing managerial personnel to attend meetings and training sessions, later to impart this information to employees who report to them.
- We may work through an employee-assistance program, addressing particular areas that seem to be the most troublesome.

This list is by no means exhaustive, only representative. It represents only some of the more obvious means to address the problem. The ways are in large measure dictated by the nature of the problem and the structure within which we must work. One company with which we are acquainted made a real effort to reach its employees, albeit on different matters and before co-dependency was even born. We want to relate that experience because we think it is one of the most creative solutions we have seen.

Example. The president and chief executive officer of a service organization decided he wanted to have more contact with employees and wanted more employee input. In order to accomplish this he interviewed a number of "experts" and got their ideas. The one he picked was unique. This particular man had spent a number of years working directly with Walt Disney. Disney had developed the "story board" concept for designing and creating some of his work. This was, according to the consultant, later adopted as a management style by Disney as well as several other major corporations. This particular organization had about two hundred employees, which made it fairly manageable. The president first arranged a Saturday meeting (not too popular) at which time the consultant explained what would be happening. (One disgruntled employee called it a bunch of "Mickey Mouse nonsense.") Nonetheless, the stage was set for the process to begin. The employees were told that each of them would be keeping their own story boards at their work stations. The story boards themselves were cork boards about two feet square, sectioned off top

117

and bottom. The top section had three blocks labeled "To Do," "Doing," and "Done." This represented the flow of work for that individual. Each employee had small pieces of paper upon which he or she could write the appropriate message and then tack them on the board. As work progressed, these messages would be changed. In this way any supervisor passing by could tell what the employee was doing. The bottom section had two parts: "Input" and "Hangups." The first was for ideas the person might have about his or her job, and the second was for problem areas in the flow of work or the job itself.

In addition, an entire room, known as the "Planning Room," was set aside in the building with large story boards in it. These were wall-mounted on slides and could be moved about. Any employee could go in and put his or her ideas on small pieces of paper and tack them on the appropriate board. Later an employee group would review these and decide which ones seemed most worthy to pursue.

There were boards primarily for input, i.e., ideas. For example, an employee might have an idea about a new marketing slogan to help sell a product. He or she would then put this idea on a piece of paper and tack it to the story board dealing perhaps with "Services." Others were used for those ideas that had been accepted and were being studied. So the idea that dealt with the new slogan might be moved to a story board labeled "Ideas Under Study." Still another board was devoted to those chosen to be put into action. If our employee's slogan was to be used further, it would go to a board entitled "To Do." If a particular project was important enough, it might be given an entire story board that would be laid out similarly to the individual ones employees kept at their desks. This would show the flow of work with respect to this particular project.

The president then met with all employees in small groups in the Planning Room. He explained his thoughts about this form of management and solicited input from all employees. This may all seem silly to some managers, but the employees in this organization had a unique experience: they had the opportunity to help chart the direction of their company with the belief, as stated by the most senior manager, that all ideas would be considered. Imagine the excitement when employees felt they were being heard and that someone actually cared about their opinions.

It takes a lot of energy to come up with a solution such as this and to follow through on it. But beyond that, it takes a major commitment on the part of management. Senior officers have to be thoroughly convinced that this is a worthwhile project before it will work. In the case example cited, the president had made his decision, and that set the tone for the rest of the company. In the final analysis it did not make so much difference how the exact technique worked and precisely what was adopted. The more important issue was that employees at all levels understood that management was interested in what they felt and thought and was willing to consider such feelings and thoughts in strategic planning for the company. This alone is enough to change the tone of a company.

Breaking the Shame Cycle. We have said a lot about shame in this work. It is the dynamo that drives most of our collective addictive behavior. Recovery means that most of us have to come up with some way to break the cycle. If we cannot do this, we will have a really difficult time completing the recovery process.

We could talk about this on an individual level for a long time. Some writers have already begun to explore this, and our purpose here is not to spend a lot of time on it. What we want to do is look specifically at an organization and try to see some of the ways in which this cycle can be broken. We would like to suggest five types of corporate acts we believe will help break this cycle.

First, it is important to try to seek out and find the source of the corporate shame. This is generally rooted in the past, although in rare cases it may be something that is occurring in the present. For example, in the latter situation if there is a president who is constantly breaking the law, or skating close to the edge, this may give employees a sense of feeling "bad" about their employer. It is much the same as if a parent is continually doing something illegal and the children know about it.

If it is something from the past, then management must try to ascertain precisely what happened. Something has caused an infection, and it is still having an effect on employees and the corporation itself. This may be hard to find in companies that do not keep complete and accurate documents. Where records are incomplete, the following may prove to be alternative sources of information:

- Retired employees and old-timers still employed
- Independent accountants
- Corporate counsel

- Minutes of the board of directors
- Directors themselves
- Minutes of committees of the board
- Management
- People in the community
- Bankers
- Trade creditors
- Large shareholders

The point of this exercise is to try to find out what has happened in the company in the past, either as a part of its official history or those unofficial and little-reported events that may have caused some sense of shame. A good signal for the investigator is to look closely at anything that was not reported or that was made a secret. These are the types of things that companies try to hide from outsiders.

Second, the person conducting this investigation must separate fact from fiction. When we begin to go back in time, there is a tendency to take legends from the past and breathe life into them, making them appear as fact today. We can do the same thing corporately. If you want an example, look at the image robber barons have today. These people were predators who quite literally stole from others. Yet today we often see them portrayed as leaders of industry, men who did great and wondrous things in a bygone age.

When the facts begin to come together, it is important to search out sources and to make certain what is being dealt with is actually fact. To the extent it is fiction this needs to be exposed. The assumptions and conclusions drawn from those fictions also need to be dealt with. This process is also sometimes painful because some of the company legend and mystique will be threatened.

Third, we need to look at the facts themselves and determine if beliefs with respect to them are rational or irrational. This may seem to be an odd process, but we do know that sometimes people attach strange meaning to real facts and come up with some very distorted beliefs. We call this cognitive distortion. There are a number of books that deal specifically with this, at least from an individual perspective (Burns 1980). We suggest that overcoming this at an organizational level is not materially different.

Some common tricks our collective minds may play on us are:

- Irrational thinking — thinking patterns most people do not have
- Catastrophisizing — taking small events and making them into something terrible
- Dealing with "should," "must," "ought to," "have to" — always placing unreasonable demands on oneself
- Feeling that outcomes will be "awful" — believing that if certain things do not happen, something terrible will follow
- Overgeneralizing — taking one episode and trying to make it into a life's pattern
- Polarized thinking — seeing things in absolute terms, black and white (Ellis 1975)

Fourth, it must be determined if there are any special factors keeping the company stuck with this type of thinking. For example, assume that the primary source of shame in the company is the founder's predatory activities many years ago and today his grandson and namesake is president of the company. The "old man" has been all but canonized by the family. It is going to be hard to overcome this obstacle and try to deal with the problems that have brought the company to its present position.

Or perhaps the myth of the company and its past represent something of present value to the company and its image in the marketplace today. Will management then be willing to sacrifice this tangible benefit for another somewhat more nebulous benefit that may await it after the change?

Finally, there may be times when the sources of shame are not known and cannot be discovered. In that case the expert will have to try to help the healing within the organization without the benefit of a purging of the past. This is best done by focusing on the benefits of the present and the hope of the future. These are two rather strong anchors to which people can attach themselves. They should be approached in the order given.

We are intent on breaking the cycle; if any of it remains, it is like an animal that regenerates itself and then reappears in some other form at another time. Most of the steps suggested are aimed at approaching the source and revealing it to the light of truth. The idea is to defuse it to the point that it no longer has any credibility. Breaking this cycle is essential to organizational recovery, and without it the following steps will not provide any lasting effect. The combination of successfully dealing with shame along with the other suggestions will speed the healing process.

Impersonality. This is a tough problem to solve, especially in a large organization. It is not really practical to request management to reach down into the rank and file in an attempt to give personal attention to employees. Impersonality must be solved in some other manner.

We liked the idea of participative management, which was introduced and fostered in the example we gave earlier. By involving employees in the decision-making process, they began to have a sense of belonging within the organization. We personally like the term "management through involvement" better since it seems more descriptive and goes a step beyond the participative type. This type of management has done a lot to dispel traditional employee ideas about whether their ideas and opinions count. And when an employee idea was adopted and made into policy, not only the initiating employee but other employees as well felt a sense of accomplishment. It was almost like they were saying, "See, we can come up with some good ideas, too."

So, first, we suggest some type of management through involvement be instituted. If this seems like an overwhelming burden, be assured that a number of authors have written about this sort of thing, and numerous companies have tried it successfully. Size does not matter, although it is usually easier to turn the company ship if it is smaller. (Interestingly, some of the worst offenders in this area are smaller organizations.) A program such as management-by-objectives can be used. In this case the company plan for the ensuing year as well as mid- and long-range planning is built from the ground up. Employees decide what their objectives will be for the coming year and then are measured both by the quality of the goals they have chosen and their performance measured by this yardstick they have crafted. These goals should not be so inflexible that they cannot be changed along with changing conditions. A quarterly review is useful in this respect.

Second, we suggest that employees be granted sabbaticals periodically, much the same as is done in academia. This is an opportunity for some personal growth and allows the employee to recharge his or her batteries for another round within the organization. This does not have to be for a long period of time. It can be as short as three or six months and still have a beneficial effect.

Third, we believe that the opportunity to participate in small group processing units within the company is helpful. In this way employees from different strata meet together periodically to discuss problems within their own areas of work as well as those they see within the company at large. This gives a chance for employee input as well as some cross-fertilization of ideas among different departments. One of the really good benefits that flows from this is that managers and executives have an opportunity to keep more in tune with what is truly happening within the company and are able to sample employee attitudes on a firsthand basis. If this is instituted, care must be given that employees are free to talk and state their opinions and ideas without any fear of reprisal. The first time reprisal happens, the system will fail.

There are unquestionably other good ideas that could be added. These are samples and are meant to be representative only. The variety of programs are limited only by the creativity of management.

Hierarchy. First, look very closely at the number and type of "perks" managerial employees receive. Are they realistic given the type of company, the profitability, and the corresponding benefits nonmanagement employees receive? If there is any question on these matters, then management should take another, closer look at these fringe benefits.

Second, we have commented in another place about the mind-set of many managers, particularly older ones, about how employees should be treated. It is much like that old parental attitude where some type of invisible line is drawn between parent and child. Managers do the same in the fear that if they begin to mix with and treat employees on a personal basis, somehow they will lose control. The saying that "Familiarity breeds contempt" is still a primary belief of many managers.

Yet managers who are confident of themselves and their ability do not have this problem and are able to mix freely with anyone in the company without fear of losing status. Since rank and all that goes with it are essentially artificial, much of the success of management depends on individual style and confidence. This type of interchange between managers and employees can benefit the company in two ways: the employees feel more a part of what is happening and less cut off from management; and the managers themselves will have better opportunities to know what is happening within their areas of responsibilities. There is something human about one person taking time to listen to another, which raises the level of interchange within the company from impersonal to at least somewhat more personal. As this happens, the idea of a hierarchical structure begins to fade.

Comparisons and Competition. It seems inevitable that there will always be competition within an organization. Earlier we noted that this is the way some rise and others fall. What concerns us is when this whole process gets out of hand.

First, it is important to set out the rules of the road for all employees. We believe that each employee needs to know what is expected in his or her job and then needs the tools and support to accomplish that work. Too often managers have some hidden agenda they want to accomplish but do not communicate this to employees. So, when the worker does not measure up, he or she is left in a state of real confusion about what happened. We have seen this frequently. Another way the supervisor can help is to give the employee constant feedback about the work, *positive* as well as negative. Employees often go for long periods of time wondering if they are doing their jobs satisfactorily, assuming that if they do not hear anything bad, it must be okay, more or less.

Second, once the rules are established, they need to be applied evenly, giving each employee the opportunity to excel and rise based upon his or her performance. Too often managers take the rules they have approved and then use them to institute a series of rewards and punishments loosely guided by such standards, but really applied on an ad hoc basis according to their own biases. Employees will generally put up with a lot if they feel they are being treated fairly. Management needs to keep a sharp lookout on this area and correct abuses immediately. There are also many legal ramifications surrounding this area today with civil rights issues, discrimination, and collective bargaining agreements. Smart management would be addressing the issue even if it were not good from the standpoint of employee morale.

Poor Communication Patterns. Volumes have been written about communication, and we do not propose to try to improve on most of that. We do want to make some specific suggestions we feel will help with co-dependency in the workplace.

The remedy to the problem lies in opening up communications within the company. Almost all of the communications issues we talked about earlier addressed ways that communication was shut off. First, what we suggest is that all forms of communication within the organization be reviewed, asking these four questions: (1) *what* is being said; (2) *how* is it being said; (3) *to whom* is it being said; and (4) what is *not* being said. As the company explores these questions, a pattern will generally begin to emerge that will serve as a base line from which to begin making changes.

When this has been established, then management needs to look at patterns to see what changes really are necessary. Second, in keeping with this, it is important to communicate with employees on a regular basis. Irregularity often breeds omission. That is, if the company is sending out regular information, it is easy to include data that comes up from time to time. Conversely, it becomes convenient to overlook, postpone, and forget important material if the communication is sporadic.

Third, wording is very important. We saw a memorandum recently where the division head started out by saying all personnel "will be required to be in attendance at each of the following meetings. NO EXCUSES WILL BE ACCEPTED." And later he continued, "I am looking forward to a pleasant working relationship with each of you." This is not calculated to make employees very happy. The whole tone is both threatening and patronizing.

Similarly, there are times when the communicator appears to be talking down to employees. For example, the division head who quotes Aristotle to assembly-line workers probably will not come across very well. This type of correspondence is arrogant, and that is the way workers will receive it.

If language is too stilted or formal, the effect is one of distancing rather than drawing closer to people. The more personalized the information is, the more acceptable it will be to the majority of employees.

Fourth, managers and supervisors need to be encouraged to keep verbal as much of their communication as possible. Writing has some shortcomings that talking does not. We see benefits to spoken communication. First, it saves time: the time it takes to dictate a memorandum, the time it takes to type it, the time it takes to reproduce it, and the time it takes to deliver it. All of this translates into costs. Second, when people talk to each other, it is much more personal and allows them to achieve a closeness they cannot have through writing. Spoken communication helps with some of the other areas of criticism we have had about management styles, e.g., hierarchy and depersonalization. Third, when people are meeting face to face, it gives the speaker the opportunity to clarify his comments and the listener the chance to give feedback. Both are great tools in communications and will help avoid many of the confusions that arise whenever two people attempt to communicate with one another. Finally, it gives managerial personnel the chance to assess employee moods and attitudes. This is not possible with anonymous communication. This may be one of the greatest benefits since it can help identify problems as they are developing rather than always having to react to them after they have become full grown.

Fifth, managers need to be trained and encouraged to listen. That sounds silly to most people, but then most people do not know how to listen. In counseling we have found the hardest thing to do is to listen carefully to what the other person is saying.

Often when people try to communicate with one another, they engage in parallel monologues. They are like two train rails, always next to each other, always moving forward, but never intersecting. One of the primary causes for this is that most people are much more intent on what they are going to say in response than listening to what the other person is saying. This intensifies if the topic is one that is critical or controversial.

Listening actively is the key that opens the door to communications. It is not nearly so important what is said, but rather what is heard. One person may feel he has said something very clearly but the other has heard something very different. Dr. M. Scott Peck talks about this in *The Road Less Traveled* and in some of his tapes. He says that when he really listens to another person giving a talk, he often will break out in a sweat and be exhausted when it is over. That is the amount of energy he puts into it.

The Spiritual Nature of Human Beings. It would be very easy to write a book about this. Remember we said earlier that we hesitated to bring up this topic since it can conjure up such negative feelings? Yet when we talk about recovery, we again realize how essential it is.

When doctors, counselors, and others, especially including Alcoholics Anonymous (A.A.), began to look at alcoholism, they realized it was a multifaceted disease, one that included both physical, mental, and spiritual dimensions. The now-famous Twelve Step program of A.A. has a spiritual basis. It has been the most successful recovery program not only for alcoholics, but also for people addicted to other things. (For a discussion of the application of the Twelve Step recovery program to corporations, see Mary Riley, *Corporate Healing*, 1990.)

There does not seem to be any real argument with this precept at this time. A.A. relied on the works of Carl Jung and William James, among others, in formulating its program of recovery (A.A. World Services, 1957, pp. 64, 68). It should not be surprising that spirituality can also be important in recovery from the addiction of co-dependence.

It is as though the spiritual nature of human beings forms an umbrella that covers all that happens in relationships within organizations. If it is missing, there can be no true recovery. If it can be found and used, it can be the bedrock from which healing grows.

We suppose first that managers must believe that people indeed have a spiritual nature and that it is important in his work. This has two parts. Many managers will probably admit that people do in fact possess some degree of spirituality, if for no other reason than it would look bad for business to profess otherwise. But there are those who will fail to see how that has any application to the business world. They will claim that sort of stuff is better left to preachers in church on Sunday.

We disagree. Spirituality reaches into all the nooks and crannies of life. We also believe that shame happens when there is a spiritual void, and that the person who is rightly centered spiritually will probably be able to avoid shame. If this is so, then spiritual growth should help rid the person and the business of co-dependence.

An average person works about 60 percent of his life, and this work consumes about one-half of his waking hours during that time. Thus, he spends roughly one-third of his life at work. That is an enormous amount of time, and it is reasonable to expect that what happens at work will have some profound effects on the quality of life as a whole. If the work experience is good, life stands a better chance of being successful.

Second, one of the primary goals of spiritual development and recovery is to help the employee end his own sense of isolation. Most co-dependent people are lonely at their core. They often surround themselves with other people, but they do not have the sense that they are accepted or fit in. They feel awkward and different.

Probably everything we have said in this chapter is pointed in this direction — the chore of making others feel like they are truly accepted. In dealing with organizational co-dependency, we want to try to find ways to make the individual employee feel as though he is a part of the business, that he can become involved in the organization in a personal, yet healthy, way. When this happens, he is able to give his best and to receive full measure of personal satisfaction for the job he has done. If he feels isolated, rejected, or betrayed by his company, he will continue in his isolation.

Third, management needs to recognize and accept the uniqueness of each person. Much of what happens in business today, especially in large organizations, tends to homogenize people. They are often looking for people to take over a job type 112 x 45, described in such and such a fashion in the employee manual. They are not looking for individuals or individuality. They want anonymous, clonelike automatons. This is especially true with assembly-line operations, which adds to the depersonalization discussed earlier. People become truly anonymous in the company, and this lack of individuality increases the sense of isolation and helps breed more co-dependency.

Individual recognition, looking for and developing employee skills other than immediate job skills, and cross-training make the employee feel more self-actuated, i.e., more fulfilled as a person, and helps the company since the employee becomes not only happier in his job, but also trained to perform other tasks if needed.

Fourth, we believe the organization should encourage creativity. This sounds strange to some people, but there are many workplaces today where creativity is viewed with suspicion. Creative people are seen as mavericks, people who do not fit neatly into the slots that have been created by management for "maximum efficiency." We think this is sad since many employees have excellent ideas about improvements in products, quality, or work flow. They have a perspective that management cannot see. They are doing battle in the trenches each day while supervisors and managers are often separated by several layers of intermediaries.

When a company accepts and encourages creativity from employees, they feel as though something inside them has been touched in a special way. They feel wanted and prized. But when this is shut off and discouraged, it is as though the inner spark has been extinguished and something that was very vital has died. Such employees become humdrum types, clones marching off to work each day.

Fifth, managers need to expect the best. A couple of examples in the text talked about those types who say they expect great things, but actually feel inside their employees will not be able to deliver. They actually expect workers to fall short or fail. This says very little about any sense of positive regard management may have for employees.

Perhaps the true issue is one of trust. We think that many managers simply do not trust their employees. Or perhaps managers do not really trust themselves. Whichever is the case, it says to workers that they are not trusted. When they get this label pinned on them, many of them will simply give up doing their best.

We think trust may be a bigger issue than most people believe. If a manager truly lacks trust, we believe he should first look within himself. Lack of trust can be a common co-dependent trait, one he may have independently or one he may have inherited from the business. If this is not the problem, then he should look to the quality of his employees.

Finally, companies whose managers look like a row of fundamentalist deacons do not leave much room for their employees to be human. Managers need to have a sense of humor. So does the organization itself. People will make mistakes because that is part of being human. Organizations themselves have the same problem periodically. The result may be some strange and wonderful, sometimes even bizarre, things that will happen in every business. The ability to laugh, especially to laugh at oneself, helps keep some sense of sanity in a sometimes crazy world.

CHAPTER 11

FINAL THOUGHTS

We have tried to give the reader a broad overview of organizational co-dependence along with some suggestions about how to deal with it. The book will hopefully spark some interest among human relations workers as well as mangers at all levels.

The real keys to opening the door to recovery lie in education of management and a willingness to begin dealing with the problem. Until that time, employees continue to be at risk. We think this problem is as serious as those addressed by laws regulating safety and health measures in the workplace. The onset of co-dependence is more insidious in most cases, but the results can be as dramatic as those of any other work-related illness or injury.

It is also our hope that someone will eventually be able to construct and carry out an experimental design that will show management conclusively that this is a dollars-and-cents issue. Perhaps the McDonnell Douglas study discussed in Appendix C might serve as a model for this.

For those of you who may be co-dependent, we wish a happy and complete recovery. For those of you who may be exposed to the challenges of organizational co-dependency, we hope you can arm yourself for survival. For managers of sick companies, we hope you can get the help your organization needs to begin healing.

APPENDIX A

DIAGNOSTIC CRITERIA
FOR CO-DEPENDENT PERSONALITY DISORDER

A. Continued investment of self-esteem in the ability to control both oneself and others in the face of serious adverse consquences.
B. Assumption of responsibility for meeting others' needs to the exclusion of acknowledging one's own.
C. Anxiety and boundary distortions around intimacy and separation.
D. Enmeshment in relationships with personality disordered, chemically dependent, other co-dependent, and/or impulse disordered individuals.
E. Three or more of the following:
    1. Excessive reliance on denial
    2. Constriction of emotions (with or without dramatic outbursts)
    3. Depression
    4. Hypervigilance
    5. Compulsions
    6. Anxiety
    7. Substance abuse
    8. Has been (or is) the victim of recurrent physical or sexual abuse
    9. Stress-related medical illnesses
    10. Has remained in a primary relationship with an active substance abuser for at least two years without seeking outside help

Used with permission, Timmen Cermak, M.D., (1986). *Diagnosing and treating co-dependence.* Minneapolis, Minn.: Johnson Institute.

APPENDIX B

CO-DEPENDENT CLIENT INDICATED AS ACCEPTABLE FOR INDIVIDUAL PSYCHOTHERAPY

1. Clients in gross crisis
2. Clinical depression
3. Excessive anxiety
4. Dual diagnosis/internal disorganization (borderline schizophrenia)
5. Adjustment problems with group psychotherapy
6. Client indicates choice for individual psychotherapy
7. PTSD prominent
8. Resistance to group
9. Person who vacillates between co-dependency and narcissistic behavior
10. Interpersonal relationships tend to be hierarchical

Used with permission, Timmen Cermak, M.D. (1991). *Adult children of alcoholics. Volume two: treatment.* Minneapolis, Minn.: Johnson Institute.

APPENDIX C

The McDonnell Douglas Corporation (MDC) of St. Louis is a $15 billion-per-year company employing over 125,000 employees. In 1985 it commissioned Alexander & Alexander Health Strategy Group to design and conduct a longitudinal study to test the cost-effectiveness of its employee assistance plan. Alexander & Alexander used 1985 as the target year and conducted a series observations from 1985 through 1988, gathering data from an EAP group and a cohort non-EAP group. The study examined claims experience and absenteeism. To be conservative, soft dollar items such as productivity, job performance level, replacement labor costs, and other subjective data were ignored.

The results were impressive. Reporting in the August 1989 issue of *The Almacan*, Alexander & Alexander stated the final cost-offset ratio (investment-to-savings) was four to one, and the total dollar savings for the EAP population over the four-year period was $5.1 million.

Source: J. Goff, 1990. "Corporate responsibilities to the addicted employee: a look at practical, legal, and ethical issues." *Labor Law Journal*, April: 214–21.

REFERENCES

A.A. World Services, Inc. (1957). *Alcoholics anonymous comes of age.* New York: A.A. World Services, Inc.

Beattie, M. (1987). *Co-dependent no more.* Center City, Minn: Hazelden Foundation.

Bradshaw, J. (1988). *Bradshaw on: healing the shame that binds you.* Deerfield Beach, Fla.: Health Communications, Inc.

———. (1988). *Bradshaw on: the family.* Deerfield Beach, Fla.: Health Communications, Inc.

Burns, D. (1980). *Feeling good. The new mood therapy.* New York: Signet Books.

Cavanaugh, E. (1989). *Understanding shame.* Minneapolis, Minn.: Johnson Institute.

Cermak, T. (1986). *Diagnosing and treating co-dependence.* Minneapolis, Minn.: Johnson Institute.

———. (1990). Workshop presentation. Johnson Institute. Houston, Tex., May 30–31.

———. (1991). *Adult children of alcoholics. Volume two: treatment.* Minneapolis, Minn.: Johnson Institute.

Ellis, A. (1975). *A new guide to rational living.* North Hollywood, Calif.: Wilshire Books.

Goff, J., and P. Goff. (1988). "Trapped in co-dependency." *Personnel Journal,* December, 50–57.

Hafen, B., et al. (1983). *Alcohol.* 2d Ed. Minneapolis, Minn.: West Publishing Co.

Johnson, V. (1980). *I'll quit tomorrow.* New York: Harper & Row.

Kubler-Ross, E. (1969). *On death and dying.* New York: Macmillan Publishing Company, Inc.

Miller, A. (1981). *Prisoners of childhood.* New York: Basic Books.

———. (1983). *For your own good.* New York: Farrar, Straus, Giroux.

Nakken, C. (1988). *The addictive personality*. Center City, Minn.: Hazelden Foundation.

Napier, A., and C. Whitaker. (1978). *The family crucible*. New York: Harper & Row.

Peck, M. S. (1978). *The road less traveled*. New York: Simon & Schuster.

Riley, M. (1990). *Corporate healing*. Deerfield Beach, Fla.: Health Communications, Inc.

Satir, V. (1972). *Peoplemaking*. Palo Alto, Calif.: Science and Behavior Books, Inc.

Schaef, A. (1987). *When society becomes an addict*. San Francisco: Harper & Row.

Siegel, B. (1986). *Love, medicine and miracles: lesson learned about self-healing from a surgeon's experience with exceptional patients*. New York: Harper & Row.

Wegscheider-Cruse, S. (1985). *Choicemaking*. Pompano Beach, Fla.: Health Communications, Inc.

Yalom, I. D. (1975). *The theory and practice of group psychotherapy*. 2d ed. New York: Basic Books.

OTHER SUGGESTED
READINGS

Abbott, S. (1985). *Co-dependency, a second-hand life*. (pamphlet) Center City, Minn.: Hazelden Foundation.

Alberti, R., and M. Emmons. (n.d.). *Your perfect right*. San Luis Obispo, Calif.: Impact Publishers.

Beattie, M. (1989). *Beyond co-dependency*. Center City, Minn.: Hazelden Foundation.

Black, C. (1981). *It will never happen to me*. Denver: M. A. C. Printing and Publishing Divisions.

Carnes, P. (1983). *Out of the shadows: understanding sexual addiction*. Irvine, Calif.: CompCare Publications.

Flax, S. (1985). "The executive addict." *Fortune*, June, 24–31.

Goff, J. (1990). "Corporate responsibilities to the addicted employee: a look at practical, legal, and ethical issues." *Labor Law Journal*, April, 214–21.

Jung, C. (1928). "The concept of the collective unconscious," in R. F. C. Hull (trans.), *Archetypes and the collective unconscious*. Bollinger Series XX. Princeton, NJ: Princeton University Press.

Kaufman, G. (1980). *Shame: the power of caring*. Cambridge, Mass.: Schenkman Books.

Larsen, E. (1985). *Stage II recovery. Life beyond addiction*. San Francisco: Harper & Row.

———. (1987). *Stage II recovery. Love beyond addiction*. San Francisco: Harper & Row.

Loveinger, J. (1976). *Ego development*. San Francisco: Josey-Bass.

Maslow, A. (1970). *Motivation and personality*. 2d ed. New York: Harper & Row.

Middleton-Moz, J. (1990). *Shame and guilt*. Deerfield Beach, Fla.: Health Communications, Inc.

Minuchin, S. (1974). *Families and family therapy*. Cambridge, Mass.: Harvard University Press.

Norwood, R. (1985). *Women who love too much*. New York: St. Martin's Press.

Rosellini, G., and M. Worden. (1987). *Here comes the sun: dealing with depression*. Center City, Minn.: Hazelden Foundation.

Schaef, A., and D. Fassel. (1988). *The addictive organization*. San Francisco: Harper & Row.

Schaef, A., and D. Fassel. (1988). "Hooked on work." *New Age Journal*, January/February, 42–63.

Sierlin, H. (1974). "Shame and guilt in family relations." *Archives of General Psychiatry*, 30, 381–89.

Trice, H., and P. Roman. (1972). *Spirits and demons at work: alcohol and other drugs on the job*. Ithaca: New York State School of Industrial and Labor Relations, Cornell University.

Weiss, L., and J. Weiss. (1989). *Recovery from co-dependency*. Deerfield Beach, Fla.: Health Communications, Inc..

Whitefield, C. (1987). *Healing the child within*. Pompano Beach Fla.: Health Communications, Inc.

Woititz, J. (1983). *Adult children of alcoholics*. Pompano Beach, Fla.: Health Communications, Inc.

———. (1985). *Struggle for intimacy*. Pompano Beach, Fla.: Health Communications, Inc.

INDEX